DON TRUM

SEEKING MY PEACE IN THE MIDST OF CONFLICT

MEMOIR OF A SOUL RESCUED BY GRACE

outskirts
press

DEDICATION

I dedicate this book to my beloved mother, Anna Belle Meade, whom I lost on October 5, 2012. A few months after Mom died, I had a dream about her. In the dream, she said to me, "Now I know why your writing means so much to you." Mom, you are and always will be, my inspiration.

This book is also dedicated to the innumerable number of men and women who have been made to feel disqualified and unworthy of being a Christian simply because of sexual orientation. Jesus died for all, that every man and woman may be a child of God. Jesus said in John 3:17, "For God sent not his Son into the world to condemn the world, but that the world through him, might be saved."

And lastly, I dedicate this book to those who have stared into the abyss of suicide. There is much to understand about the suicidal mind, and I hope through this book and the courage of others who have survived suicide, that we may bring greater light to penetrate the darkness.

Table of Contents

FOREWORD

Don Truman Wilson tells well here his personal story of coming to grips with the conflict between his once-loved Pentecostal Christianity and his once-latent homosexuality. Attempted suicide was the turning point. No longer a closeted gay man, neither is he a gay activist.

Like most of the rest of us, Don would like to get on with his life, accepted if not celebrated, being both loved and loving. As he has changed from a timid child to a confident man, Don has learned much, and the reader will share in that education.

One sage remarked on the value of learning from mistakes, preferably those made by others. Mistakes like Don's ill-considered marriage to a much-older woman who wanted to "make a man" of him, but not a gay man.

You will come away from reading this book with an enhanced understanding of the conflict between certain Christian denominations and their homosexual members. You will admire the transition of the author from insecure to secure, from puzzled to aware.

We are instructed to love our neighbors. Well, some of our neighbors are gay, and we are to love them, too…platonically, at least.

Douglas Winslow Cooper, Ph.D.

douglas@tingandi.com

WriteYourBookWithMe.com

Walden, NY

Spring 2020

ACKNOWLEDGMENTS

I thank my coach and editor, Douglas Winslow Cooper, Ph.D., for his help and friendship. Doug Cooper is known as "the completionist" because he helps writers get their books finished. Doug came into my life at just the appointed time. Thank you, Doug, for believing in me!

I gratefully acknowledge the life-saving work of the American Foundation for Suicide Prevention (AFSP), and I thank the Central Florida Chapter, who took me under their wings when my life was fragile.

I am indebted to Linda Joy Myers, Ph.D., M.F.T., the President and Founder of the National Association of Memoir Writers, namw.org. Linda is the author of *The Power of Memoir—How to Write Your Healing Story,* and of the workbook, *Journey of Memoir—The Three Stages of Memoir Writing.*

I thank Brooke Warner, publisher of She Writes Press and SparkPress, president of Warner Coaching, Inc., and author of *Write on, Sisters!; Green-light Your Book; What's Your Book?* and three books on memoirs.

I gratefully acknowledge the influence of Jerry Waxler, M.S., the author of *Memoir Revolution: A Social and Literary Shift that Uses Your Story to Heal, Connect and Inspire.* His blog, www.memorywritersnetwork. com/blog, started in 2007, contains about 400 essays, interviews, and reviews about memoirs.

To the Institute for Writers, formerly the Long Ridge Writers Group, Madison, CT: as a graduate of their program, I want to thank them for each instructor I was privileged to work with.

I especially thank Tilar Mazzeo, Ph.D., for her lectures, "Writing Creative Nonfiction," for *The Great Courses*. My writing would not be what it is today without her expertise and instruction in writing prose.

I thank my sister, Diane Wilson-Perry, for her confidence in me and her inspiration to finish this memoir. I love you, Sis!

PREFACE

"O, God, I have tasted Thy goodness, and it has both satisfied me and made me thirsty for more. I am painfully conscious of my need for further grace." Pastor A. W. TOZER (1901-1963)

We can best comfort others by giving the comfort we ourselves have received. As the theme of my memoir – being at peace amid conflict – conveys, our personal peace can be attained even in life's heaviest burdens.

For years I believed same-sex attractions were damning, that for me just to be attracted to another man was a sin. As I white-knuckled my way through the decades of the 1980s and 90s, fasting, praying, and many times even having hands laid on me to deliver me from a supposed demonic spirit of lust, I eventually wore myself out trying to be worthy of God's grace.

There is something wrong with a Christian doctrine where the teaching makes the disciple's hate turn inward. Many a time as I struggled against my same-sex attractions, I came to the point where I loathed my body for what I perceived were sinful desires, and ultimately, I hated my life as well. Self-hatred became a slippery slope toward suicide.

My motivation for writing this memoir is two-fold.

First, I want to show other gay men and women that there is nothing wrong with being gay, and it's time to stop seeing ourselves as if something were wrong. God has made us in His own image, and He saw that it was good.

Second, I want to give hope to the individuals who might have come to the wrong conclusion because of self-hatred, that life is not worth living. Life is worth living. You are a beautiful creation, unique in every way. If someone has a problem with who and what you are, it's their problem, not yours. We must stop living our lives to please others. When we don't put such limits on ourselves, we will live much happier lives.

My own suicide attempt was a wake-up call. For too many years there was no joy in my life because I had no self-esteem. There was only self-loathing. After my suicide attempt, I was forced to explore not only what was wrong in my life, but also, what was right. I began to see being a gay man as a good thing.

A proverb says, "Just when the caterpillar thought its life was over, it became a butterfly." On that fateful near-death evening in 2009, I honestly thought my life was over. I had no desire to go on living. But as I lay there on my bed after taking an overdose of pills, hoping to drift into unconsciousness and death, my faith in God spoke new life to my being. God had a bigger plan for me than I had ever imagined. From that pit of despair to where I am today, I have come to see each new day as a gift.

I hope through the words I have written someone will gain hope from my experience and find new meaning in life. Film producer and musician, Tom Hiddleston wrote, "You never know what's around the corner. It could be everything. Or it could be nothing. You keep putting one foot in front of the other, and then one day you look back and you've climbed a mountain."

Please, don't ever give up. I promise it does get better!

"Life is either a daring adventure or nothing at all," Helen Keller wrote. As I climbed out of that pit of despair over ten years ago to where I am today, I would have never dreamed that one day I would jump out of a perfectly good airplane at 18,000 feet. Judy Blume in her novel, *Tiger Eyes*, wrote, "Each of us must confront our own fears, must come face-to-face with them. How we handle our fears will determine where we go with the rest of our lives. To experience adventure or to be limited by the fear of it."

Welcome to my world. Let's choose to experience the adventure together.

Don T. Wilson

Spring 2020

INTRODUCTION

At the age of twelve, I knew I was gay. Although not fully able to comprehend all the ramifications of such an identity, at this young age I began a journey of mixed emotions, contradictions, confusion.

It was also at this tender age when I first became aware of the presence of God. Just a few years before, when attending vacation *Bible* school at a large Baptist church, I had a schoolboy's knowledge of God and the teachings of Christ, but it wasn't until I began to attend The Second Presbyterian Church in Huntington, West Virginia, that the reality of God's presence penetrated my heart.

Having a more personal experience with my Creator was exciting for a twelve-year-old. I was even allowed to join a youth choir at this Presbyterian church. Learning to sing opened the door for me to sing at a church service for my Grandpa Truman at my grandparents' house before he died in 1973. I will always treasure this memory.

One of my earliest memories of Sunday school in this Presbyterian Church was hearing about a trip our Sunday school teacher had taken to the Holy Land. The teacher was Clarence Huffman. Clarence was instrumental in planting the seeds of faith in my young heart. One

Sunday morning, Clarence brought in some movie slides he and his wife had taken on their recent trip. He was excited to share their experience with the Sunday school class. The whole class was excited to see pictures of this sacred land where Jesus had walked and lived. The slides made an impression on me. The scenes of the Dead Sea, the Sea of Galilee, Nazareth, depicting the land surrounding Israel, brought my faith to life.

Now, many decades later, as I reflect on how that knowledge of God has structured my life, I have come to realize how all the experiences with my faith over the years, put together like a jigsaw puzzle, have made me the man I am today.

Throughout the storms of my life, enduring many years of conflict and torture in my mind while attempting to reconcile both my faith and my being gay, surviving a suicide attempt in 2009, and most significantly, experiencing the sudden death of my precious mother in 2012, I have come to realize just how vitally important faith is to my life. One cannot experience life-changing events such as these without undergoing metamorphoses.

Since I overcame my suicide attempt in January of 2009, my life has been an amazing quest. In late 2010, I became involved with the American Foundation for Suicide Prevention (AFSP). In June of 2011, I traveled to Boston to attend a symposium on suicide prevention in gay youth. This symposium left an indelible mark on my heart. Noting a rash of suicides related to bullying issues over the last few years, I felt I needed to take a stronger stand, and I have continued to be involved with the Foundation for Suicide Prevention. This participation has brought me a brand-new purpose in life.

Today, I am much more aware of suicide causation and prevention than ever before. The subject has mesmerized me. I will always be thankful for getting involved with the American Foundation for

Suicide Prevention. In fact, the organization has an annual "Walk Out of Darkness" here in Orlando on the first Saturday of each February that I participate in to raise awareness for suicide prevention, one of my life's chief goals.

One of the purposes in writing my memoir, *Seeking My Peace in the Midst of Conflict*, is to educate the public about what it's like to struggle with homosexuality as a Christian, and also to help my readers better understand the human psyche and how it responds to years of intense mental conflict. The reader will be introduced to a psychiatric term called "psychache," an unbearable pain in the mind. The term was coined by the late Edwin Schneidman, in his book, *Suicide as Psychache*. They will read and come to understand my dealings with psychache and how I overcame it.

One of my favorite quotes is from Philip Yancey's book, *Disappointment with God*. It reads, "Faith means believing in advance what will only make sense in reverse." As I try to make sense of some of my struggles, most notably trying to reconcile my Christian faith with being gay, I have often wanted to know the answer to "Why?" But "Why?" is one of the age-old mysteries we face with God, His ways being inscrutable.

A quote from C. S. Lewis's *A Grief Observed* sums it up succinctly: "When you are happy, so happy you have no sense of needing Him, so happy that you are tempted to feel His claims upon you as an interruption, if you remember yourself and turn to Him with gratitude and praise, you will be—or so it feels—welcomed with opened arms. But go to Him when your need is desperate, when all other help is vain, and what do you find? A door slammed in your face, and a sound of bolting and double-bolting on the inside. After that, silence."

A walk with God demands faith. As *Hebrews 11*:1 tells us, "Faith is the substance of things hoped for, the evidence of things not seen."

Looking at my life through the lens of faith has made me realize that oftentimes life doesn't make sense. From a different perspective, I'm seeing my life as though looking at the back of a tapestry. The pieces may not all make sense throughout the different stages of my life, but one day, when the time is right, I will have gained the perspective from which the woven pattern will be a masterpiece of intricately laced details.

Today, I look to the future with an exuberance of hope and joy, a lively hope I am excited to share with others who may themselves be struggling with conflicts of their faith, similar to my own dynamic quandary between Christianity and homosexuality.

PROLOGUE

CONTEMPLATING SUICIDE

Finally, on a Saturday evening in January 2009, realizing I could no longer endure the angst of a fractured relationship and a conflicted mind, I staggered my way through the dense fog of my emotions to our upstairs bedroom.

Without a doubt, to contemplate suicide has to be one of the darkest experiences a human heart can know, a moment of incredible loneliness. You feel abandoned by everyone, even God, as if alone in the universe.

The moment to end my life had come. My tormented soul would find peace at last. When a suicidal person makes it to this juncture, it is all but finalized. In his mind, it is settled. For him to execute this final act of misery will be easy. His relief is in sight. He doesn't see the devastating effects the act will have on his family and friends. He only wants the unbearable emotional pain to end.

I had mulled the final act over several times. I decided upon an overdose of pain pills. As I stood motionless at the bathroom sink, the blank face in the mirror resembled my own. Because of the long-term emotional pain of the conflict, I had lost my desire to live. As I took one last look at the person who stared back at me, I lifted the hand that held the pills, and I thought to myself, "so this is how it ends."

Seconds crept by. I put the handful of pills into my shaking hand. I took a deep breath, swallowed the lethal meds with a gulp of water, then stood silent for the longest time, no emotions---no fear, if anything, relief. I staggered over to my bed in a daze, the ache of my heart accompanied by such loneliness I had never felt.

PART I
A CHILDHOOD SURPRISE

CHAPTER 1

MY FIRST TWELVE YEARS

On the 23rd of June 1960, Dad worked as a welder on a high-rise hotel in Cleveland, Ohio. Suddenly, his foreman yelled up to him that morning, "Jerd, how many boys do you have?"

"I have three," Dad answered.

"No, you have four. Now get to the hospital!"

I was born in Elyria, Ohio, a 23-mile jaunt from Cleveland, in Elyria Memorial Hospital. I already had three older brothers: Rodney, Kayo, and Harold. Now they had a baby brother to play with.

Mom and Dad, Anna Belle and James Reed Jordan Wilson, were both reared in central West Virginia, Clay County. They had married before Dad joined the army, around 1951. After Dad returned from Japan in 1953, having been a corporal in the Korean Conflict, they moved from Clay County, WV, to northern Ohio after my brother Rodney was born, so Dad could find work as a welder, a trade he had learned in the army.

My older brothers, Kayo and Harold, were born in Medina County,

OH, in Lodi. Not long after I was born, the family moved back to West Virginia.

There was a huge factory in Huntington, WV, American Car and Foundry (ACF Industries). Dad found employment there as a welder around 1963.

In the winter of 1963, while Dad worked in Huntington, Mom and we four boys lived up in a hollow in a small house, in Maysel, WV, Clay County, owned by a Mr. Vaughn.

On a brutally cold morning, with ice encasing all the windows, Mr. Vaughn walked slowly up to the house and cautiously knocked on the door. Afraid we had all frozen to death, he was relieved when Mom answered the door. To Mr. Vaughn's surprise, Mom had built a fire in a coal stove and had us all huddled around the stove to keep warm.

My mom, Anna Belle, knew what it took to protect and care for her four boys. In the years to follow, she would forge a bond so deep with her four, soon to be five, children that would never be broken. Anna Belle instilled a deep love and respect in all of them, love and respect that endure until this day.

Sometime before June of 1964, Mom and we four boys joined Dad in Huntington, WV. On June 29th, 1964, Mom gave birth to her only daughter, Diane Daisy. Our family became complete. My earliest recollection of Diane is seeing her in her bassinette as a baby, with pink bows in her hair.

I can remember to this day the house we lived in back in the middle 60s. In the yard stood a tall weeping willow tree. I remember distinctly a thunderstorm one summer evening with the wind and rain blowing the tree limbs back and forth and breaking a lot of tree limbs. I can also remember the sound of locusts as they rubbed their wings together on a summer evening, nesting in that same weeping willow tree.

One day when my brothers were at school, I happened to be climbing around on the back porch when I slipped and caught my left arm on an awning hook. Mom hurriedly made a tourniquet and summoned one of our neighbors and took me to the hospital.

Although she had baby Diane to take care of, her little boy Don was always getting into mischief. Another mischievous antic little Don got into was on the same back porch. Mom had a wringer washing machine. One day while she was doing some laundry, Don in his own way of trying to help his mommy, got his arm caught in the wringer. Mom had to stop the washing machine before Don's arm was too badly hurt.

In my early years of grade school, I was so attached to my mommy that it was difficult for me to be out of her sight to attend school, Head Start, or first grade. What the cause of this was, I don't know. The emotional attachment became so severe in the first grade that I cried incessantly when I had to leave her when she would take me to school.

On one occasion, as she was on her way back to the school I attended, the mailman asked her, "Going to get Don again?" He had seen her time and again on her way to get me.

In the years to follow, my strong bond with my mother would be forged. A name I soon acquired was "Annie's Little Shadow."

The separation anxiety became so bad that I missed a lot of school in the first grade, and for this reason, I failed the first grade. Mom was my refuge, my shelter, my protector. I eventually grew out of this separation anxiety period, but it would take a couple of years. I've often wondered if this has anything to do my being a gay man. I had a much stronger mother-son relationship than I did a father-son relationship.

CHAPTER 2

A HOUSE DIVIDED

As elementary school advanced into junior high, the separation anxiety I felt toward Mom subsided. There were more dire circumstances to worry about. The atmosphere at home during those early years was filled with vulgarities and senseless quarrels. Dad wasn't a happy drunk; he was a mean drunk. The fights between him and Mom often escalated into violence.

One of my favorite passages by the great theologian, C. S. Lewis, is from his masterpiece, *Mere Christianity*. These words have profoundly affected me,

"But if you are a poor creature—poisoned by a wretched upbringing in some house full of vulgar jealousies and senseless quarrels—saddled by no choice of your own, with some loathsome sexual perversion—nagged day in and day out by an inferiority complex that makes you snap at your best friends—do not despair. He knows all about it. You are one of the poor whom He blessed. He knows what a wretched machine you are trying to drive. Keep on. Do what you can. One day He will fling it on the scrapheap and give you a new one. And then you may astonish us all—not least yourself: for you have learned your driving in a hard school."

On one occasion, probably when I was about ten, one of their fights became so violent, I distinctly remember Mom's becoming hysterical, possibly because she had too much to drink, I'm not sure, and an ambulance had to take her to the psychiatric ward of a hospital. In my mind, I can still see the neighbors all out on their porches as the ambulance took my mom away. The embarrassment I felt only added to the resentment that was beginning to form a scab in my heart towards my dad. I think it is safe to say that after all the quarrels and fighting between Dad and Mom, it's no wonder there wasn't any love lost between me and Dad.

Whether Dad did not really love me as his son or I simply refused his love, I don't know. I do know it's very important for a father to have a good relationship with his son, and vice versa, and when this relationship is less than satisfactory, deep-seated problems can arise. I've often wondered if my strained relationship with Dad had any bearing on my sexual orientation.

Although there were good memories of Dad's taking us boys to a Cincinnati Reds game, as I grew older, the resentment toward him had already made its mark. As I moved into my teenage years, the tension was so bad between Dad and me, it was hard for both of us to be in the same room. Dad was a man's man so to speak. An army veteran. A tough exterior. Perhaps he knew his youngest son was gay. He did call me a "queer" once, when I was about fifteen. This only added to the antagonistic relationship we had. The ironic twist about him and me is: I look just like him. He was a good-looking man. A lady's man for sure. I'm proud to look like my dad. In all honesty, I've always wished we had gotten along better. Who knows? If he had lived, perhaps we would have.

My relationship with Mom was always good. In my mind, she could do no wrong. Don't get me wrong, Mom was no saint, but she knew what it took to hold our family together, and she always went the extra mile to do just that. She loved us all with such unconditional love, and this love was so strong, that it afforded us all the security we needed.

I remember when Mom went forward in an altar call and gave her heart to the Lord. There was a beautiful change in my mother. She would get all dressed up to go to church. I was so proud of her. Unfortunately, it wasn't long before Dad, in his twisted alcoholic mind, began to accuse her of having an affair with the preacher. This jealousy on Dad's part made it very difficult for Mom to enjoy her walk with the Lord. Although she would be strong in her faith, her Christian life was fraught with demons of strife and jealousy.

My relationship with my three older brothers was good: they were my protectors.

I have always had an enduring and endearing relationship with my sister, Diane, up to the present day. I thank God for her. There is a special bond between us. Although we would fight like cats and dogs when we were young, I always missed her when she wasn't around. On one occasion, she had gone to visit one of Dad's brothers and his wife in northern Ohio. I remember looking at one of the pictures of us together and crying because I missed her. This is the love we still share.

We don't get to choose the family we're born into, but honestly, I don't have any regrets about the family I was born in. Even with all the conflicts and strife I've experienced with Dad, I am the person I am because of God's grace molding me.

CHAPTER 3

SEXUAL AWAKENING AT 13

Cary's musky scent lingered in the autumn breeze. I had met him a few weeks earlier but never thought much about him until that summer afternoon in 1973 when I turned 13. Suddenly, his masculine physique, tanned legs, hairy chest, and curly Afro, awakened an unfamiliar passion in me.

As he and I explored the grounds of a vacant house in the neighborhood, his manly scent seduced me into an almost drunkenness. My pulse raced. A swift adrenaline rush sent my hormones into a frenzy. Instinctively, I inched closer to him, to seize any chance I had to softly touch his olive skin. As his silky, chest hair glistened in the afternoon sun, this uncharted territory I found myself in seemed natural.

A young boy caught in the jaws of puberty, until then I hadn't noticed the sexual aspect of my existence. I had dated one girl, and even though we wore each other's wrist bands and kissed a lot, my awakened sex drive on this summer day with this older guy of 17, cast me into surprising flames of eroticism.

Cary no doubt sensed my stirred passions. He asked me if I wanted to go see his bedroom. Like a puppy, I followed him up to his bedroom where he lived in a half-way house just across the street. Once inside his bedroom, he locked the door. Though he was older than I and taller – I might have been 4'11" – I felt safe.

Here I was, an adolescent, age 13, locked in a bedroom with a virile man of 17. After a few minutes of showing me his aquarium, he asked me what I would like to do. Without hesitation, I said, "let's wrestle." I longed to touch his body, feel him against me. My sexual energy had been awakened, and there was nothing to stop the aroused passions.

Cary, at his discretion, lay on his bed as I climbed on top of him. I had never experienced another man in this manner, touching his strong arms, feeling his hairy arms and chest. I was enraptured by this mulatto. We wrestled for a few minutes to the point where I had a sexual release, almost to the point of embarrassment. He must have known, though no words were ever spoken. He just smiled.

I didn't see Cary again until many years later after this interlude of intimacy, and when I did, I wasn't sure if he remembered me, but the image of him and me on his bed has stayed with me. Occasionally, I will get a whiff of his scent, and it will take me back to that time of innocence and awakening at 13.

To this day, I'm greatly attracted to mulatto men, as well as Middle Eastern men, virile and hairy. I'm confident it's because of this sexual awakening as a young teen to a man of mixed race.

PART II
SCHOOL DAZE

CHAPTER 4

MIDDLE SCHOOL/
HIGH SCHOOL

The idiom from our childhood, "sticks and stones may break my bones (but words will never hurt me)" is a chant I remember well, one event in particular.

The playground bustled with other children at play. Screams of laughter echoed throughout the schoolyard on this bright and sunny morning. I was twelve, midway through my sixth grade at Johnston Elementary in Huntington, WV, a city situated on the Ohio River, bordering the states of Kentucky and Ohio. The year was 1972; early spring, the air still cold. Although many classmates played nearby, I stood alone when it happened: a moment etched in my memory forever.

Swiftly, Roberta raced up to where I stood, and without saying a word, delivered a fierce slap to my face. The force of the slap jolted me, like waves pounding the shore. The imprint of her hand reddened across my face. Stunned, I was speechless. There was silence. I couldn't speak. Humiliated right there in front of the whole class, I felt reduced to a grain of sand.

Although I had been acquainted with Roberta through our interactions in class, I wasn't aware she knew who I was. She did! For some reason, I had made an enemy. What had I done? What had initiated the attack?

For days, the shock and bewilderment of that slap affected me. With my emotions inflamed, I felt humiliated and embarrassed. A feeling of scorned had taken control of my emotions.

A few days before this traumatic event, Johnston Elementary had held its annual Spelling Bee, an event I looked forward to each year. During the Spelling Bee that year, after several rounds, the contest dwindled to two opponents, a classmate of mine, Robert, and me. Robert was a tall boy for his age, with glasses. I, your average student, small in stature, stood barely four feet eleven inches.

The tension was thick in the auditorium this particular afternoon. You could almost cut it with a knife. Robert and I went several rounds before he stumbled on an unfamiliar word. (The rules in Spelling Bees state that if a contestant misspells a word, his opponent must then spell the word correctly before being declared the winner.) When I did spell the word correctly, I was declared the winner. After that was announced, a hush fell over the crowd. There had been an upset.

The repercussions from defeating the school ace, Robert, in the Spelling Bee, would reverberate for some time. Roberta's act of retribution gave this bully the last word. She was going to show this new hotshot, me, exactly how she felt about defeating her school favorite.

This playground assault dealt my self-esteem a big blow. Formerly a fragile, perhaps cowardly person, I was now even more so. I then faced a brand-new challenge in life, an unfamiliar new tempest, in the form of a girl.

Consequently, the only recollection I have of that fateful sixth-grade class at Johnston Elementary way back in 1972 was that climactic event on the playground. The scene branded my psyche and haunted me for many years to come.

Bullying is terrible. The smack I encountered on the playground back in 1972 contained the essence of bullying, and it hurt.

The act of bullying itself has been around for thousands of years. We can see bullying at its infancy in the Garden of Eden. In *Genesis 4* we have an account of two brothers, Cain and Abel. Cain is a tiller of the land, and Abel tended the flocks.

Over time, as the writer of Genesis tells us, Cain brought some of the fruits of the soil as an offering to the Lord. Abel also brought an offering—fat portions from some of the firstborn of his flock.

In this narrative, we see that the Lord found favor on Abel and his offering, but on Cain and his offering, the Lord did not look with favor. So, Cain was very angry, and his countenance fell. Then the Lord said to Cain, "Why are you angry? Why is your countenance fallen? If you do what is right, will you not be accepted? But if you do not do what is right, sin is crouching at your door; it desires to have you, but you must master it."

Sometime later, mankind's first murder takes place. Cain suggests to his brother Abel, "Let's go out to the field." While they were in the field, Cain rose and attacked his brother and killed him. We can only speculate why Cain slew Abel. Most likely it was because Cain's offering was rejected by the Lord. Only what is written here in *Genesis* Chapter 4 tells us.

One previous encounter with belittling that sticks out in my mind happened in gym class when I was in the fifth grade at Monroe Elementary, back in 1971, a year earlier. It happened during gym class one afternoon. Monroe was an average-size elementary school. The gymnasium also was used as a lunchroom. After the students were excused from lunch and the afternoon bell had rung, the gymnasium was transformed into an arena of sorts for basketball and gym class.

This particular gym class consisted of about 20 students; we were told that we were going to test our climbing abilities by scaling this rope hanging from a steel beam. My being close to eleven years old, I was a very shy, puny kid, barely four feet eleven inches in height at this point. I knew that scaling this rope was going to be a monumental task for someone my size. I can distinctly remember thinking they were all going to make fun of me. *They will all laugh at me.* My self-confidence when doing sports activities was always very low. I was not the athletic type. Who knows why I always felt so inferior? The puzzle pieces to this riddle would only begin to make sense a couple of years later.

On this particular afternoon, even after only a few minutes, when it was obvious to the other kids that I was having a very difficult time climbing the rope, some of the kids began to jeer, to mock me. Other boys whom I had already tried to befriend, even they were calling me names. Words such as "sissy" and "weakling" were hurled at me. The pain I felt was all too real.

West Junior High School was large. I once again would be reunited with friends I had gone to Monroe Elementary with, before attending Johnston Elementary in the latter part of the sixth grade. It was also here at West Junior where I would begin to notice something in my life a bit more paradoxical, my attraction to the same sex. Here I was, a boy just entering his teenage years, and I was noticing not girls, but other boys. Although to me it was natural, I knew from the derogatory names other boys who were like me were called, that to like other boys was not the most popular thing. There were consequences to being different, and it wasn't too long before the name-calling and periods of rejection would arise again.

Entering junior high school became a challenge for me. I would now be attending West Junior High School on the west side of Huntington. The year was 1973, a very critical time in the United States. The Watergate scandal was at its peak. Even in a small town like Huntington, tongues wagged about the perplexities of this issue.

My memories of West Junior are not all bad. I joined the Glee Club in the eighth grade, which in itself helped to solidify my acceptance at this big school. There would be other circumstances, however, which would cause the bullying issue to once again emerge.

The gym class at West Junior was a struggle for me. Having low self-esteem, to begin with, I often felt rejected, humiliated when the last one picked for a team.

Although this happened several times, one time it affected me the most. In the first half-year of the seventh grade, two of us were left who hadn't been chosen for a team.

You could hear the kids who had been chosen yelling, "Pick her! Pick her!" Finally, after the last captain chose my girl classmate, I remember walking slowly over to the other team feeling like a whipped puppy, rejected. I had been chosen to be on a team...by default.

Labeled a sissy for many years, I was begun to wonder, did I play sports that badly? Why was I being called this insulting name? What did it all mean? I started to question my masculinity at this point. The cancer of self-doubt began to eat away at me.

In her profound, song-writing masterpiece, "At Seventeen," Janis Ian conveys how hurtful a young person's life can feel:

> To those of us who knew the pain
> Of Valentines that never came
> And those whose names were never called

When choosing sides for basketball.

A strange thing happened one afternoon at West Junior High School in the latter part of my seventh grade. Two classmates of mine, Jim and Tim, who had bullied me for years, suddenly befriended me. Stunned, I wondered *what had happened?* What I didn't know was, my brother, Harold, a "hood", a tough character who hung out in the alley in the back of the school on breaks, had somehow made it known to these two 'bullies' that he was Don's brother. After finding this out, the two bullies made an about-face. They could no longer mistreat Harold's little brother, for fear of incurring his wrath.

After these incidents, I knew I had to find something, a sport, an event that I could excel at, some way to fit in with the other kids. My self-esteem needed a boost. I was desperate.

I began to explore bowling. My mom, being one of the chief cooks at one of the large bowling alleys in Huntington, would allow me to go to the bowling alley each day after school. Being an employee's son, I could bowl for a quarter a game, a bargain.

Sometimes, I would be asked to do certain chores, such as sharpening pencils and cleaning league scoring mats. Back in the early-to-mid-70s, the custom was to mark a bowler's scoring on plastic placards. I would clean these placards with a soft cloth, erasing the white markings. I was always willing to do anything I was asked to do, to earn coupons so I could bowl. I had found my niche! Quickly, I realized bowling was something I could excel in. Before long I was joining a bowling league, competing in tournaments, both city and state, vying for trophies.

Finding bowling as something I could throw myself into helped me tremendously in coming out of the shell that I had retreated into because of past experiences with bullying.

To my surprise, West Junior High School had formed a bowling team.

When I heard about this, I jumped at the chance to prove I had at least one sport I was good at. If my memory is correct, our team did very well. And I met some very good friends as a result.

As a result of this bowling team, I continued to bowl into my early 20s with great success. I bowled my high game of 258 in 1982.

MY FIRST CRUSH

The Merriam-Webster Dictionary defines "crush" (noun) as, "a strong feeling of romantic love for someone that is usually not expressed and does not last a long time." Some crushes do last longer than others, however.

My first crush on another guy hit me like a ton of bricks: Joe was a classmate of mine in Typing II class during my sophomore year at Huntington High School. Joe was a very likable guy, very popular with the girls in the class.

Each day I entered Typing II Class, my eyes would immediately search for him. There he'd be, smiling innocently, sitting at a desk directly behind me, waiting for the class to begin. This guy with curly blond hair and blue eyes had cast a spell on me. One look at him was all it took to make my day. If he smiled at me, even better.

How was I supposed to react to this massive crush that had engulfed me? There was no roadmap to guide me in the ways of young infatuation and romance, especially towards members of the same sex. I was riding a topsy-turvy emotional roller coaster, my emotions in an uproar. Their furor astonished me! I had never experienced such amorous feelings toward another guy.

This was all new to me, yet, very real, incredibly genuine, natural. At a time in life when most guys are having their first crush on girls, here

I was having a crush on another guy.

In time, however, the experience left me feeling empty, alone. Somehow, I knew this head-over-heels crush on Joe was one-sided. As much as I wanted his affection, it never came. Even though the crush on Joe was one-sided, that didn't stop these relentless feelings. Wave after wave of emotions washed over me day after day, as though the floodgates had opened at Hoover Dam, with torrents of water sweeping everything out of their path.

One cannot simply turn off feelings of such an intense infatuation, as one would a light switch, no matter how hard one tries! I was enamored, infatuated with Joe and thought about him constantly. What was so different about him from other guys? Why did he have such an effect on me?

O, the heartache of unrequited love! *The Urban Dictionary* defines unrequited love as the feeling of being completely, hopelessly, desperately in love with someone, all the while knowing that your feelings will never reach this person. I doubt Joe knew I existed. He never gave me a second thought. Infatuation was entirely mine; my thinking conjured up the fantasy of romance between us.

How could I have a crush on someone I only saw once a day in a typing class? That's the powerful subtlety of infatuation: infatuations are real, gladly / sadly / bittersweetly real.

The tide of infatuation with Joe eventually receded during my sophomore year, but the memory of that one experience has endured.

RIDICULE IN THE LIBRARY

According to the Wiktionary, the fear of being ridiculed is known as "catagelophobia." Few people get through life without being mocked or teased, but most are confident enough to cope with it: for those with this phobia, being laughed at is one of the worst things that can happen to them.

During my junior high and senior high school years, I was no stranger to ridicule. On one occasion in my junior year at Huntington High School back in 1977, an all too memorable incident of ridicule happened one afternoon in the school library. I had always enjoyed reading, so being in the library was not unusual. On this particular day, I was sitting alone at a table when three classmates of mine walked in and sat at a table adjoining mine. The library was quite empty. Perhaps these bullies expected this. Oftentimes, bullies will single their victims out privately.

Although I knew of these guys, I was not in their inner circle of friends. Huntington High was a very large high school, comprised of students from different junior high schools. The student body was broken into many cliques. I was not part of this clique, nor any clique for that matter. I do remember two of these guys were twin brothers, Kevin and Kerry, and the other guy was a school jock, Dane, a very attractive guy.

I can't quite recall exactly how the events unfolded, but I do remember that after they had been sitting for a while, I overheard the three of them snickering. At first, I wasn't sure what they were snickering about, so I just ignored it. However, when the snickering continued, and I glanced their way, I could make out Dane's scornfully winking at me. He would wink, and then they would laugh, then he would wink again. This went on for several minutes. It wasn't long before I realized that they were having fun with mockery at my expense. Their sarcastic snickering made it all too clear that this wink was not a flirting wink. They had chosen me as their object of ridicule.

I got up from my chair and left the library. I scurried out as fast as I could, like a whipped puppy with its tail between its legs. Their on-slaught of ridicule had left another mark on my already wounded spirit.

DAD'S DEATH IN MY TENTH GRADE

My sophomore year at Huntington High School, in 1976, would be a year of many changes and realizations. Most importantly, in November of that year, my dad, only 48 years old at the time, suffered a fatal heart attack in his sleep. This devastated much of the family, especially Mom. Although she and Dad had divorced a couple of years before, there remained a deep love for each other.

I will never forget the shock my precious mom and older brother Stan experienced that dreadful day. Mom received a phone call from the lady Dad rented from, telling Mom that Dad "looked funny" and that she thought maybe something was wrong.

Mom handed the phone to my brother Stan, and this lady asked him, "What should I do?"

Being asked this, Stan became livid. He couldn't understand why this lady hadn't called for an ambulance before calling us. Stan next, in anger and disbelief, ordered her to call for an ambulance.

He immediately drove Mom, as fast as he could, to the east end of Huntington, where Dad lived (a distance of approximately three miles). Upon arriving at his apartment, they were met by paramedics, who told them Dad had already been pronounced dead.

Stan, always very close to my dad, was devastated. I could never fully comprehend the impact this chain of events must have had upon him. I remember Stan and Mom were both overcome with grief upon arriving back at our house that fateful November 1976 evening. Even to this day, this one moment remains a memory forever etched in my mind.

On that November day so many years ago, with Mom and Stan returning home, I immediately made my way out to the back of the house, wanting to be alone. I still recall the cold, bleak weather of that November day. Light snow flurries were beginning to fall from the ashen sky. The coldness was numbing. All at once, there was a stillness I hadn't experienced, as if the world suddenly stood still. I felt confused, but at the same time, relieved.

I tried to cry, but no tears ever came. Why couldn't I cry? I had just lost my dad, a figure who to many sons is their whole world, their hero. Had the resentment that had been buried in my heart for so many years towards this man finally exerted its full effect? Did I hate this man, whom I called "Daddy," so much? Could I be glad my alcoholic father had died?

I was the youngest boy of four boys. Dad and I had never gotten along very well. We could hardly stand to be together in the same room. My relationship with Dad hadn't soured overnight. It had taken many years for the love between us to grow cold. Alcoholism destroyed our family. The disease had ruined his and Mom's marriage. We five children had suffered the explosions and implosions of this sickness. His drunken outbursts and fights had left me incapable of loving him.

The man who at times was to me, a monster, was gone. My jaded memory was filled with alcohol-filled nights when he and Mom would fight, often to the point that Mom would become hysterical, sometimes having to be taken by ambulance to the hospital.

How vividly I recall so many times after these outbursts had occurred, that the neighbors would be out on their porches gawking at all the commotion. I endured such embarrassment! Now, looking back on all this upheaval, is it no wonder that I couldn't shed a tear when this man died?

As I had alluded to earlier from the verses of the nursery rhyme, "Sticks and Stones," I recalled, "Sticks and stones may break my bones, but words will never hurt me." Yet, I remember an occasion when I was about fifteen, perhaps a year before his death, when Dad had called me a "queer." This accusation cut me to the quick. At an age when I couldn't comprehend the changes puberty was impressing on me, not least my sexual orientation, how the hell was I to understand such a derogatory word being hurled at me from my father? This insult just added to the many layers of negative emotion I already felt toward this man.

Now, so many years later, I wonder, could I have ever loved this man I called "Daddy"? Had I ever really tried to love him? Had he ever tried to love me? When a son truly loves his father, the relationship has been nourished, layer upon layer, over some time, usually many years. Although there were a few good times with Dad, going to a Cincinnati Reds game one weekend, his taking me to the Tri-State Airport once in Huntington to visit the weather bureau, the resentment and disdain I felt toward him destroyed any chance of loving him.

Adding a bit of irony to the dissimilarities Dad and I had, the one incredible fact is: I look just like him. Of all five of children conceived by him and my mother, Anna Belle, I'm the one who resembles him the most. Coincidentally, once while visiting one of his sisters, she had commented to me on how much I looked like Jerd (a nickname Dad had acquired). I remember thanking her for the compliment. Surprisingly, I was proud to look like this man. He was considered a very handsome man. He had very strong facial features, piercing blue eyes, qualities I've been blessed with.

To this day, in my heart of hearts, I wish my relationship with Dad had been better. I guess every boy who hasn't gotten along well with his father wishes this. On many occasions, I have visited his grave on Wilson Ridge, in central West Virginia, and silently tried to grieve. I regret that I cannot.

No matter how hard I try, tears for Dad just won't come.

PART III
A CAREER OF SORTS

CHAPTER 5

ALMOST A JOURNALIST

As I reeled from two dynamic forces in my life that senior year of high school, it's no wonder the path of my future was uncertain. I was confused and bewildered over the loss of a dad I resented, a father I couldn't mourn the loss of; at the same time, I found myself attracted to other boys, instead of girls. With such dilemmas, it's hard to make wise decisions about one's future endeavors.

At the end of my junior year, I could have graduated, but I lacked an English credit. This forced me to go my whole senior year to acquire the credit. Always interested in the media, especially the genre of music, I took an elective in journalism that senior year. Journalism proved to be a good choice, for it allowed me to share my interests from music and entertainment.

I had always been a fan of Casey Kasem's "American Top 40." This count-down was broadcast on a local radio station, WKEE in Huntington, each Sunday noon. I seldom missed a broadcast. The radio station gave a listener each week the chance to win the four-album recording. One week, my name was chosen. I never felt so excited.

The Huntington High School newspaper was *The Tatler*. In the journalism class that senior year, I was allowed to write a column for each edition of *The Tatler*. I chose to write a review column of the past few months from *Billboard Magazine*'s "Hot 100 Singles" and "Top 200 Albums." I felt so privileged and excited to share something that was of keen interest to me.

I had been purchasing *Billboard Magazine* at a local newsstand in Huntington, Nick's News, for about a year. So, my back issues, along with segments from Casey Kasem's "American Top 40," gave me the resources I needed to write the column.

The opportunity to write this monthly column awakened a desire to write. Little did I know that some thirty years later, I would pursue a writing career.

The column in *The Tatler* was well received. If my memory is correct, a guy whom I knew from the class decided to continue the column the next year.

My home life didn't afford me a conducive atmosphere for studying. Despite this unsettled environment, I had always managed to score above-average grades. When I entered high school, I had signed up for college prep classes.

The year that Dad died, 1976, I had Mr. B for "Biology with Laboratory," and he was probably the most difficult biology teacher at Huntington High. I also had his wife, Mrs. B, for Spanish II. I passed both classes marginally. I'll never forget the compassion both Mr. and Mrs. B showed me that year when the man I called "Dad," died. Written on my final grades by both, was the word, "conditional."

My math and science aptitudes were not as strong as other subjects, such as English composition, for example. So, after taking the ACT exam, I might have allowed this to deter me from pursuing college at the university level. Because, after graduation from high school, I decided to go in a different direction. I chose to attend a business college instead of Marshall University in Huntington. I did graduate the diploma program with a degree in accounting.

Though I would later attend Marshall University, taking a few courses here and there, I regretted not pursuing journalism. I had no idea at the time what God had in store for my life. As I look back, it all makes sense. My favorite Christian writer, Philip Yancey, once wrote, "Faith means believing in advance what will only make sense in reverse."

As I look back over those turbulent and indecisive years of the late 1970s and early 1980s, I do not fully understand what steered me away from journalism, but I am thankful the desire to write has never left me.

I would often write a column in my hometown newspaper, *The Herald-Dispatch*, to voice my opinion on many issues throughout the 1980s. The column was called, "The Voice of the People." I still have some of these clippings, and I am thankful I used that opportunity to explore the field of journalism in the editorial/opinion domain.

George Eliot, a/k/a Ann Evans, wrote, "It's never too late to be what you might have been." Sometimes life has a way of going full circle. In my life, what I once thought might have been a journalist career detoured into accounting and even the ministry, but now has almost come full circle.

As I pursue the field of writing, as an author, I often tell friends that when I'm writing, especially scenes for my memoir, it feels like a seed budding deep in my heart. Never, ever, give up on your dreams I tell them.

"Too low they build who build beneath the stars," wrote the eighteen-century poet and theologian Edward Young. The nineteen-century English poet Robert Browning expressed a similar opinion,

Ah, but a man's reach should exceed his grasp,

Else, what's a heaven for?

Just so.

CHAPTER 6

COMING OUT

A GUY WHO WHISTLED

The early 1980s were years of growth and discovery for me. In 1982, I finally passed my driver's test, after failing it twice when I was sixteen. Some drivers aren't mature enough to drive at sixteen. I was one of them. I will never forget that day I passed; I felt the weight of the world fall off my shoulder.

My early 20s were also a period of great discovery. Although I had a sexual awakening at 13, it would be many years later when I would get up the courage to act on this awakened sexual identity. It was also around this time when my brother, Stan, would have a profound dream about me, telling him that I was gay.

In 1981, I lived within a block of a gay bar in Huntington, the South Seas Lounge. Although as green as the green grass at this time in my knowledge of the gay lifestyle, I had a curiosity to meet another guy who was gay.

On a rainy night, as I walked back home from a 7-11-type carry-out,

I distinctly heard someone whistle at me. Though I was tantalized and fearful, my curiosity got the better of me. I backtracked about 500 feet. I remember seeing this guy, around my height, curly hair, attractive.

When I asked him if he whistled, he said, "Yeah."

Too scared to question the guy any further, I left him standing there and ran.

When I reached home on that rainy night, I regretted that I didn't get to know the guy, so I decided to go back to the carry-out. Hoping the guy would still be in the area, I looked fervently for him, even to the point of asking the owner of the carry-out if he had seen him. Although the owner remembered him, I was never able to find the guy. I have always wondered what would have happened if I dared to get to know this mystery man who whistled at me in a dark parking lot back in 1981.

After dinner one evening in 1981, when I was twenty-one, my older brother Stan, Mom, and I were driving home; I was in the back seat. Stan broke the silence as he began to relate a dream he'd had about me.

In this dream, he and I are seated around Mom's dining room table with a bright light shining on me. "Illuminated in this bright, white light, you break the news to us that you're gay."

For a few seconds in the car, our silence was deafening, tension thick enough to cut with a knife. After a few moments, the stillness was shattered when my brother Stan said to me, "Don, if you ever feel like you want to tell us something like this, always feel you can."

Dumbfounded, I was speechless for several minutes. Then, after mulling over what to say, I blurted out, "I am gay, Mom and Stan." Silence filled the car for the remainder of the ride home.

Whew! I instantly felt the weight of the world lifted from my shoulders. For years I'd wanted to tell Mom I was gay. Now she knew.

Not a word was spoken during the remainder of the night about the explosive revelation of my homosexuality. Ashamed to look at either one of them, I made myself scarce.

The next morning dawned in a blanket of dread for me. Restlessness prevailed.

I loved Mom more than anything in the world. Now, I sensed a great gulf between us. My tears welled up. *How could I hurt the most important person in my life? How could I ever look at her again?*

When I mustered up enough nerve to look at her, distance triumphed. She exhibited a far-away look, dazed and confused. I was convinced I had let her down; my heart was breaking.

At first, conversation dragged between us.

Mom later told me how confused and bewildered she felt that first couple of days after the ordeal. "I felt like I just existed," she said, "like enveloped in a thick fog. I couldn't move."

Even so, within a couple of days, our conversation had become lighter and normal once again.

In the coming years, I would learn the depths of this mother's love for her son.

In the early 1980s, after coming out to my family, I was desperate to meet other gay men. Lonely, and in need of affection from another man, I wasn't sure how to go about meeting anyone. Often, in our lives, desperate times call for desperate measures.

About a block from where I lived was a gay bar, South Seas Lounge. Though I was curious, I was too green and timid to dare go in. On a rainy, dark evening, as I walked home from a 7-11-type carry-out store right next to the bar, I mustered the courage to approach a couple leaving the bar. At first, taken aback, but seeing the desperation in my face, they took my phone number and told me they would be in touch. Their names were M and R. In a day or two, I received a call from Joe, who said he was a friend of M and R.

Joe and I talked a few times on the phone before we agreed to meet at South Seas Lounge one evening. Honestly, I was petrified to go into a gay bar. Whether embarrassed, or what, I don't know, but back in that day there was such a stigma about being a gay person.

The evening for me to meet Joe, I parked my car and lurched to the lounge's door. Once inside, I was okay. This first act of courage was a huge step in my coming-out process, opening the door for many other "first steps" in my early days as an openly gay man.

That momentous night, I not only met Joe but also became better acquainted with M and R, who were also at the bar that night. I must have been an obvious newbie because the owner of the bar announced that I had won a bottle of wine. It was this night that I met the guy with whom I would have my first date as a gay man.

I never did get to know Joe well, but he was instrumental in my coming-out process.

Over the next year, M, R, and I became close friends. Through them, I was introduced to other friends who helped to form my early identity as a gay man.

I grew in leaps and bounds in those days, both in coming to terms with my sexual orientation and with the discovery of a spiritual side of me, seeking Christ. The time would also see the birth of a conflict, a tortured mind.

On a bitterly cold winter night in 1981, I befriended a guy at the YMCA in Huntington. Though strongly attracted to L, he was a married man, and I dared not cross that line. We at once became close friends. And even though I developed a strong crush on him, nothing came of it. This friendship would prove to be instrumental in guiding me towards an encounter with Christ in my early 20s.

L invited me to a revival service at his church. I'll never forget that Sunday morning, as I drove up Fifth Avenue in Huntington, tears rolling down my face, wanting to give my heart to Christ. A side of me had been awakened that I hadn't known. Although I had learned of the teachings of Christ in a Presbyterian Church as a young boy, I had never been fully awakened by the Holy Spirit.

At an altar bench at the First Church of the Nazarene in Huntington, WV, on that Sunday morning in 1981, I knelt and gave my heart to Christ. The next Sunday morning I was baptized. You might say I had a new birth. I began to attend *Bible* studies, study the *Bible*, especially the Gospels, and learn to pray.

One of my favorite memories happened on Wednesday night prayer meetings. Before the pastor would share the scripture for the night, he would ask if any parishioners would like to testify. All at once, hands would pop up all over the congregation. L would testify, his twin brother G would testify of God's grace and how much he loved the old hymn, "Blessed Assurance." I can still remember the words to this precious hymn, 'Blessed assurance Jesus is mine, oh what a foretaste of glory divine, Heir of salvation, purchase of mine, born of his spirit, washed in his blood." Many of my friends there at First Church would testify on these Wednesday nights.

These were glorious days, the early 80s when I first met Christ. It didn't take long, however, to realize this new-found faith would prove to be antagonistic toward my being a gay man. It all started with my friend L, then his brother G, and so on. I was told I had to make a choice, that one cannot serve two masters. The decision was a difficult one.

My friends M and R didn't take too kindly to my new-found "religion" as they would call it. They didn't have a problem with being gay, nor did they allow religion to interfere with their sexual orientation. This proved to be a quandary for me.

Little did I know at the time, but I wasn't the only one in my circle of friends who had a conflict with being gay/being a Christian. As it turned out, L and his brother both had the same conflict.

A popular movie at this time was the controversial film, *Making Love*. The movie starred Kate Jackson, Harry Hamlin, and Michael Ontkean. The movie portrays a couple, Doctor Zack (Michael Ontkean) who is happily married to television executive Claire (Kate Jackson), but he finds himself struggling with his increasing attraction to other men. These feelings boil over when he meets a new patient, the openly gay and hedonistic Bart (Hamlin), with whom he begins a tempestuous and emotionally draining affair. His infidelity throws Zack and Claire's marriage into turmoil at a time when they had been discussing starting a family. (Source: Google)

L and I, with another friend who struggled with the same dilemma, decided to go see the film at the local theater. The effect on all three of us was traumatic.

To this day, the film touches a deep chord in my heart. Not long ago during one of my trips to Huntington, I decided to visit my ex-wife's,

M's, grave. While at the gravesite, I played the song from the film, "Making Love," as sung by Roberta Flack. The lyrics include,

Here no more confusion, we see our lives.

We live our lives.

Remember when we thought

We never would survive,

But now neither one of us is breaking.

(Songwriters: Burt N. Bacharach/Carole N. Bayer-Sager/Bruce Roberts/Bruce N. Roberts)

Within a year or so after my experience in the Nazarene church, I had stopped attending church. I soon fell back into my old habits of loose living. Although the Lord would again apprehend me in the early part of 1983, this experience with a holiness doctrine would serve to be a foretaste of things to come in the Pentecostal church.

Towards the end of 1982, after seeing all I felt I wanted to see of the gay lifestyle, I came across Tim LaHaye's book, *What Everyone Should Know About Homosexuality.* I read this book with great fervor. In the back of the book, there was a prayer for anyone longing to walk away from the gay life. After I had prayed the prayer with as much sincerity as I could, I wrote to Tim LaHaye. Within a few days, I received information about outreach in Fairmont, WV, where I could go for three days and receive counseling and spiritual guidance. It was an eye-opening time for me. I met J. He had been immersed in the gay lifestyle, but supposedly had been saved and set free from the bondage of the so-called sin. I met and counseled with J and was given fresh hope that I could live a life free of homosexuality too, as he did.

While in Fairmont, I experienced the Holy Spirit as I had never experienced before. This would be a foretaste of blessings to come in my life from the Third Person of the Trinity.

The experience at Fairmont proved to be instrumental in my beginning to attend the Pentecostal denomination, the Church of God, in the early part of 1983. The weekend that I left the outreach in Fairmont, WV, I knew I was coming back to Huntington and would start attending the Church of God.

CHAPTER 7

MY LONGEVITY IN THE WORKFORCE

In the spring of 1981, after I had completed a diploma degree program in accounting at a business college in Huntington, WV, I was hired on at a large law firm in the city, HBBP&C, as a clerk/runner, a position I would hold for 13 years until October of 1994.

I'm an extrovert, so it was not hard for me to become acquainted with strangers or new co-workers. When I first started at HBBP&C, it didn't take long for me to befriend several at the firm: secretaries, bookkeepers, etc. The bookkeeper at the firm, whom I'll call "Marie," and I are still close friends to this day.

I jumped with both feet into the workforce. Having never worked in an office setting, I obtained experience of working with attorneys that I continue to use now with the firm I work for in Orlando, FL. Office etiquette and genuine good manners go a long way in a law firm of any size.

For the first five years in this first position, I was in charge of picking up the mail at the post office for the firm every morning. Then I would sort the mail and deliver it to the attorneys, a position I enjoyed. Other duties of the job included errands to the courthouse, occasional hand deliveries to other law offices, and filing.

In 1986, the firm moved from its small office to a much larger office complex, in part due to growth. At this time, I became the firm's librarian. The firm's law library held all of the regional *Reporters*, from the *Northeastern Reporter, First Edition,* to the *Pacific Reporter, First Edition,* to the *Federal Reporter* and *Federal Supplement.* I was in charge of managing this huge, 25,000-volume law library.

One of the joys of my job as a librarian was that the position afforded me the luxury of getting to know what area of law an attorney specialized in. Back in the early 1990s, the Americans with Disability Act was being implemented. As the firm did a lot of work for corporations in the employment discrimination field, this was a hot topic. One attorney, I'll call her "Jan," did a lot of research in this area. I highly respected Jan. She and I are friends to this day.

Each year the firm would hire law students to clerk in their second and third year of law school. I got to know many of the clerks, as they would spend a lot of time in the library doing research. One student I'll never forget always greeted me with a handshake. *A really nice guy* I thought. However, when he passed the bar and came on as an associate, no more handshakes. Maybe he thought he was too good to do that anymore, I don't know. It's sad, and even though I respect attorneys and admire them for the career placement they have achieved, they are no better than I am.

There are many attorneys with whom I am friends to this day, attorneys who never lost their humanity and humility. I have more respect for these attorneys than I could ever have the ones who lack respect for their fellow man.

On the morning of October 31st, 1994, after having worked for the firm for 13 years, I came to my office to find a letter addressed, "Personal and Confidential, Only to Be Opened by D. T. Wilson." A little confused by this salutation, I at once felt the Lord remind me of *Isaiah 30*, verses 20-21, "Although the Lord gives you the bread of adversity and the waters of affliction, your teachers will be hidden no more; with your own eyes you will see them. Whether you turn to the right or to the left, your ears will hear a voice behind you, saying, 'This is the way; walk in it.'"

I knew at once the Lord was preparing me for what lay ahead. This letter accused me of deeds left undone in managing of the library; the author of the letter was the Administrator of the firm, a man who never showed me any friendliness whatsoever. After confronting him about the letter, I decided to go straight to one of the senior partners whom I knew quite well. Though T's hands were somewhat tied, he didn't want to lose me as an employee. I remember how he commented on my faithfulness over the 13 years. To make a long story short, the salary for my position had capped, and they didn't intend to pay me any more than I was making. The writing was on the wall. The Lord had prepared me for a new beginning, a new vocation in my life. Weighing the financial ramifications, I then chose to allow the firm to fire me; there was no way I was going to quit.

Overall, this proved to be a period of professional growth for me. In my personal life, I had growth issues as well. I was losing devotion to the concept of being ex-gay or, at least, trying not to be gay. We all would rather stay in our comfort zones in life. But that doesn't help us to grow. We need to sprout our wings, get out of our comfort zones in order to be the persons of growth we are meant to be.

Eventually, I moved on. In June of 1995, I was hired by Cardinal Healthcare as a customer service specialist for a nuclear-medicines pharmacy. In this position, I assisted the pharmacist in the preparation and delivery of nuclear medicines to local and state hospitals and medical facilities. Each year, all employees were trained in radiation safety and training. I held this position for seven years, until early 2003, when I moved to Florida.

I drove many miles in the seven years I worked for Cardinal Healthcare. A few times had things been a little different, I might not be here.

Early one morning after I left Huntington, and it had rained all night, I drove up Route 2 out of Huntington toward Point Pleasant, along the Ohio River. Not too far up Route 2, I saw ahead of me red lights motioning me to stop. Upon stopping, I asked, "What's wrong?"

"The road is flooded up ahead," a man said.

"How deep is it?" I asked.

"We're not sure, but I wouldn't chance it," he replied.

At the time, I worked for a hard-nosed pharmacist. He was a badass, you might say. He wanted every one of his drivers to be on time, never late. On this particular morning, I was already running late on my deliveries. So, what did I do? I did something really stupid; I decided to drive through the water that covered the road. Probably one of the dumbest things I've ever done in my life.

I drove a Ford Ranger Pick-Up that morning, a truck that was high off the ground. Who knows, this could have been what saved me from being washed away, for as I drove through the water, not once did the truck sway. To say I was lucky on that morning is a gross understatement. I finished my deliveries that morning with no other problems.

One other time as I drove a company truck for the company, I was on the West Virginia Turnpike. I remember distinctly it was 1:31 a.m. As I drove down this dark stretch of highway, probably 65 mph, a possum ran out in front of me. Instinctively, I tried to stop. I'll never forget it;

the Ford Ranger's tires felt like they began to jump down the highway as I gained control of the truck. Another close call.

On this morning, with the snow falling ever so lightly, and as I drove close to 40 – 45 miles per hour, the truck I drove began to slide back and forth, and before I knew it, I had slid off the road and came within about 100 feet from a railroad track.

Right then and there, I decided to look to the southern skies and move to Florida.

I am thankful for the opportunity I've had over the years to show long, consistent tenure in the job market. I have been blessed. I often tell people that while it's important to like the people you work with, it's maybe more important that your fellow employers like you, and they have.

CHAPTER 8

MY PENTECOSTAL PROBLEM

The late Steve Jobs wrote, "Don't be trapped by dogma – which is living with the results of other people's thinking."

From early 1983 until the early 1990s, and even somewhat to this day, my mind, my thinking, has been trapped by dogma, caught up in trying to live my life as the result of other people's thinking and convictions.

In today's world, we have church doctrines often built upon one single verse of the *Bible*. Some denominations tell you you're not a Christian unless you are baptized, denominations that say you're not "saved" unless you have been baptized and speak in tongues. Then some churches teach that once you are saved, you are always saved. On the other hand, some churches say you can backslide and lose your salvation. I simply anchor my faith in Christ Jesus, trusting his word where it says in *Romans 4:5*, "But to him that worketh not but believeth on him that justifieth the ungodly, his faith is counted for righteousness."

During a time in my life, I worried fervently about backsliding, always afraid I was going to go one sin too far and be cast into Hell. This continued for many years when I was in the Pentecostal church. If I did sin, I would be so overcome with guilt that I would almost, as saints did in the *Old Testament*, don sackcloth and ashes and mourn for a week.

I'm not saying repentance is not important; I am saying Christians are not under condemnation. Jesus took our condemnation upon Himself on the cross. And besides, the apostle Paul wrote to the Romans in *Romans 8:1*, "There is therefore now no condemnation to those who are in Christ Jesus, who walk not after the flesh but after the spirit."

The majority of Pentecostal denominations I have attended maintain that you can lose your salvation by falling back into sin. I had a very close friend who saw me struggling with this doctrine of backsliding. He asked me, "Don, what would it mean to you if you knew you could never lose your salvation?"

I said, "Chris, I would sleep a lot better at night."

Christians are not meant to walk through life with the burden of whether they can lose their salvation. In the book of *Jude*, verse 24, Jude says, "Now unto him that is able to keep you from falling, and to present you faultless before the presence of his glory with exceeding joy." Does this sound like a doctrine where one can lose their salvation? No! I serve a God Who is able to keep me from falling.

I don't want to sound like I'm at odds with all the Pentecostal beliefs; there are some godly people in these churches. I am echoing Steve Jobs's comment, "Don't be trapped by dogma – which is living with the results of other people's thinking." Our salvation is safe and secure in Jesus. In *John 10:28*, Jesus says, "And I give unto them eternal life; they shall never perish, neither shall any man pluck them out of my hand." Don't allow church doctrines to dictate your way of life. Always align with the words Jesus spoke and taught.

Stay close to God. As the writer of *Psalm 73* writes in verse 28, "But it is good for me to draw near to God."

I am convinced that if we truly love the things of God, and love God, through Christ, we are secure in His hand.

If we are truly in Christ, we will love and promote the teaching He taught while He was on this earth. Heed Christ's Sermon on the Mount, for example, from *Matthew 5: 3-6*, "Blessed are the poor in spirit: for theirs is the kingdom of Heaven. Blessed are they that mourn: for they shall be comforted. Blessed are the meek: for they shall inherit the Earth. Blessed are they which do hunger and thirst after righteousness: for they shall be filled."

The one secret is to stay close to God. Dr. Martyn Lloyd-Jones, in his classic *Faith on Trial*, wrote, "The one secret is to stay close to God. If we fail, we are like a ship that loses sight of the North Star. If we lose our bearings, we must not be surprised at the circumstances."

CHAPTER 9

1983-91, CELIBACY (EX-GAY PERIOD); MINISTRY

THE TEMPTATION

In 1984, my faith continued to grow in leaps and bounds as I appeared to get the upper hand in my war against same-sex attractions. I felt more in control than ever before.

Persuaded by a new wave of teaching taking the country by storm, the Ex-Gay movement, with the promise that homosexuality can be altered, I zealously welcomed the opportunity to change. I felt guilt and internal conflict about who I was for so long, I welcomed some kind of possible healing and shift.

My instruction with Pentecostal disciplines such as prayer and fasting at the large Church of God in West Huntington continued to reinforce my life as an ex-gay. Immersed in an indoctrination where to be gay or at best, to participate in homosexual activities, is a damning sin, I was further admonished to separate from the gay lifestyle in whatever measure deemed necessary. Rigorous *Bible* study, coupled with fervent prayer life, was highly encouraged to live a victorious Christian life. I was urged to pray and memorize scripture.

The 700 Club, a Christian organization, was invited to the church to conduct a workshop to equip those interested to be trained counselors for their 1-800-free-call-in counseling center. I jumped at the chance to prepare myself to help others.

On the morning of the first session, I was seated with my friend Jean, a woman in the church who had taken me under her wing. To my surprise, I caught sight of a handsome guy seated a couple of pews in front of me. My eyes were drawn to him. My heart racing, I fidgeted, and my palms sweated. My old sinful nature had awakened. Captivated by this unknown person, I felt a sudden rush of virility from him, and I was drawn to his masculine demeanor.

In a momentary relapse, I let my thoughts go amok. Sensual thoughts and desire for another man engulfed me. Then, in a flash, I was quickened by the teachings about temptations toward the same sex and how unnatural they are.

Immediately, my confidence in the ability to overcome these temptations disappeared.

I cried out to God to help me. "I'm sorry, Lord, I pray."

I promised to be stronger. I felt strengthened almost immediately.

Seated beside me, Jean picked up on my discomfiture. "Are you okay?"

"I am fine." At a break later that morning, I was surprised when she told me how she knew how upset the attraction to David affected me.

AN UNEXPECTED CALLING

The sanctuary was bursting at the seams that Saturday night of the revival meeting in 1985. On each side of the altar, men and women sought God, pouring their hearts out to Him in prayer and worship. It was as if an angel had taken his scepter and touched the altar and it exploded.

I had sat captivated by the evangelist's sermon, feeding on every word. When it came time for the altar service, I scanned the altar to see if there was anyone I could pray with. Almost immediately I spotted Mike kneeling there, one of my best friends.

Seated only a few feet from the altar, I hurried over to where Mike prayed. As I put my hand on Mike's shoulder to ask God to strengthen him, it happened: an event so momentous the very foundation of my being was shaken.

In a loud voice, the Holy Spirit spoke to me, "I have called you to preach; that's why your faith has been tried."

Perplexed at hearing God's voice, I stumbled back to my seat in a daze; I sat awe-struck for the longest time. After the service, I met a few friends at a local restaurant for a bite to eat. I had been fasting for three days, so I was famished. Afterward, I hightailed it home. I just wanted to be alone. I didn't mention a word to anyone about what had transpired at the altar. I pondered the experience in my heart.

I had already accepted Christ as my personal Savior in January of 1983. After attending the Church of God, a Pentecostal church, for several months, I had ardently sought the baptism with the Holy Spirit, an experience prevalent in Pentecostal churches. The experience is described in detail in the *Book of Acts* in *The New Testament*, chapter 2, verse 4, "And they were all filled with the Holy Ghost, and began to speak with other tongues, as the Spirit gave them utterance."

At a Friday night prayer meeting on June 24th, 1984, as I knelt at the altar, I distinctly heard the Holy Ghost give me the utterance to speak this heavenly language. As I began to speak the words He had uttered, the words flowing out of my body like rivers of living waters. I trembled. I had received this heavenly gift just as *Acts* 2:4 had described.

At this Church of God, I attended, it was not uncommon for the "gift of tongues" and interpretation to be operated by the Holy Spirit. On a weeknight during a revival in 1985, toward the end of the service as I was interceding in prayer for a friend of mine, suddenly, as if the burden I felt for this loved one had forcefully come up out of my belly, I opened my mouth and yielded to the Holy Spirit as He spoke a message of tongues to the congregation. The message was with such force, it nearly took my breath. Shortly thereafter, an interpretation of this message "in tongues" was given by our pastor, thus fulfilling the scripture as it is written in *I Corinthians*, chapters 12 and 14.

Bringing forth this message in tongues left me awestruck. The anointing I felt as the Holy Spirit spoke through me was one of great wonder and fear, for I had a glimpse into the spiritual world, a place where I was both astonished and taken aback.

The two years before hearing the Holy Spirit's voice calling me to preach the gospel, my faith had been severely tried. There were times when I was beset by perplexing thoughts of unbelief, thoughts such as *what if there is no God?* would harass me. Doubt and unbelief almost paralyzed me at times. I battled these demons many times, yet my faith upheld me.

In the three days of fasting before I heard the Lord's voice at the altar, I had sensed an urgency to fast. I had asked a very good friend of mine in the church if she would join me in this three-day fast. She agreed. I had fasted one or two meals before, but never fasted for this long. Our purpose in fasting was to see souls saved and brought to Christ.

This fast K and I joined in was an absolute fast, meaning we only drank water for its duration. The first day of the three-day fast is usually the hardest, as your body yields to the fast. It is crucial to keep hydrated during this time.

At this time, I was a file clerk for a large law firm in Huntington, West Virginia, and my duties were quite strenuous. I can still clearly remember the effects of this fast on my body. I was noticeably weaker. But through prayer and devotion to the Lord, I was able to focus on the purposes of the fast, helping me to accomplish what I had started.

On that eventful Saturday night, as I placed my hand on my friend Mike's shoulder at the altar, I realized my life gained new meaning. I took the seriousness of this calling of God with great fear. For it is written in the Book of Romans, chapter 11, verse 29, "The gifts and calling of God are without repentance." Meaning: once you have received a calling from God, it is always there.

The impact of being called to preach didn't fully affect me until the next morning after the evangelist preached his sermon. He had preached on the apostle Paul's being converted on the road to Damascus, as told in the Book of Acts in The New Testament, chapter 9, 1-15. Here, we read of the apostle Paul, who at the time was known as "Saul," a persecutor of Christians. As he journeys to Damascus to, no doubt, persecute more Christians, suddenly there shines a light from heaven around about him. He falls to the earth, and he hears a voice speak to him, "Saul, Saul, why do you persecute me?"

And Saul says, "Who art thou, Lord?"

.And the Lord replies, "I am Jesus whom thou persecute."

This sermon affected me with such intensity that I wept almost uncontrollably as it was preached. I remember talking after the service to my friend K, who had been fasting with me, and confiding to her what had transpired the night before. I will never forget her telling me, "Don, just take things slow." She had sensed for a long time I had been called to preach.

After the service, I shared the news with another very good friend of mine and his wife. Earl possessed a lot of godly wisdom. I looked up to him. After they had come by my apartment to talk and had gone, I felt an urgency to pray. I got down on my knees and cried out to God, "Lord, how could you use someone like me, of all people? I am most unworthy."

I sobbed.

MINISTERIAL INTERNSHIP PROGRAM

The calling to preach the gospel of Jesus Christ hit me hard. Though I felt humbled by the calling, I wanted with all that was in me to do the calling justice and to live a consecrated life that the Church of God had projected.

In the fall of 1987, I applied to a program in the Church of God known as "The Ministerial Internship Program." The program was developed for men and women who felt a calling in their lives to preach the gospel of Jesus Christ. I applied and was accepted.

The program was an intensive seven-month study of church doctrine and *Bible* study. It required the student to read through the entire *Bible* as well as a curriculum of different books on Church of God doctrine.

After I had been accepted into the program, I was assigned to serve alongside a pastor of a Church of God in Kenova, WV. Though this church had a distinction of being a legalistic church, I didn't let that deter me.

The pastor I was assigned to and I hit it off right off. He was a digni-fied man; in my eyes, a man of great integrity, especially in the Church of God. Not too long after being assigned to his church, I was given the opportunity to preach my first sermon. I will never forget the experience.

On a Sunday night, maybe a couple of weeks after I had begun at-tending, I had prepared one of the first sermons I was to preach. The sermon was titled, "The Certainty of Divine Judgment." I had sought God's will on the sermon, and as I remember, the sermon came to me most divinely, word by word. It was as if I sat down at the typewriter and bled.

I took my text from *Romans 2*. The apostle Paul is writing to the church at Rome. He is instructing his followers in Christ to be careful not to judge others when at the same time, they are committing the same sins.

The sermon was well received in our church that night. In fact, Pastor P later told me it one of the most powerful he had heard on that text of scripture.

For the seven months, I attended the Kenova Church of God, each month I would drive to Beckley, WV, for testing and fellowship with other ministers in the program. This opened the door for new friend-ships, some friendships I still enjoy up to this day.

After completing the program, I participated in a graduation cere-mony in Cleveland, TX, the headquarters of the Church of God. The culmination of the seven months of intensive study was a great ac-complishment for all of us who had pledged our lives and commitment to the Lord.

A couple of months after I had completed the training program, I was ready to take the exam for the first stage of license in the Church of God. This was called the "Exhorter's Exam." I'll never forget the morning I arrived to take the exam. Hands all sweaty, nervous, yet also a feeling of supernatural confidence.

I had studied for this exam like no other exam in my life. It was vitally important that I show myself approved for the ministry. I'll never forget how I started the exam, a series of essay questions, multiple-choice, and church doctrine. Possibly because I had studied well, I don't know, but I kept thinking to myself, *Is this it?*

The exam was nothing like I thought it would be. It was relatively easy. After I had taken the exam and walked out of the exam room, it wasn't long before one of the ministers called my name. I had scored one of the highest scores, 92 %.

With the door wide open for me to minister in the Church of God, it was as if I failed to remember the other part of me that stayed hidden from sight, that secret part of me that longed for the touch of another man.

No matter how many times I had fasted, prayed, had hands laid on me for deliverance from supposed evil spirits of lust, the temptation and desire for another man were still there. And although I would minister the gospel of Jesus Christ in the Church of God for a couple of years, it wasn't long before the demons I had fought so long to overcome came knocking at my door once more.

A COLLAPSE IN JUDGMENT

After a rigorous eight years of intense prayer and fasting, in my effort to overcome my homosexual desires, I was at the end of my rope.

My flesh was tired, my mind weary, and despite valiant attempts at reclaimed victories after stumbles to temptation, my suppressed sexual desires were at a breaking point.

Inflaming the fires of temptation, I began to purchase men's workout magazines with images of glossy, virile male athletes in skimpy work-out gear; it was a way to satisfy my bent-up lust for the male physique. It was just a matter of time before the walls of my fortress of faith would come crashing down.

Then it happened: M, a man a little older than I. He stood about 5'9", dark brown eyes, masculine, and quite handsome. I'd known him through his employer and a mutual friend. We had met once before at a family gathering. He didn't keep his sexual orientation a secret, and this intrigued me. I was desperate to get acquainted with him; so, I devised a plan.

During a week, the scene was set to make my move. One afternoon while at his store, I introduced myself and told him I was a friend of his brother's wife. Suddenly, he said, "I remember you. You attend Jefferson Avenue with Kay."

I responded with, "Yes, that's right." After this short introduction, I confessed that I needed to talk to someone about a personal conflict I was having in my life. Although I didn't go into any detail, it seemed he knew. He said something like, "I'm confident I can help."

After we chatted for a few minutes about life in general, to my delight, he assured me that anytime I needed to talk, we could meet for cof-fee; I was even welcome to come by his house. Instantly, I felt the rush of enthusiasm I hadn't felt in a long time.

"What evening are you free?" I asked excitedly.

"I am free tomorrow evening," he replied.

Before I could respond, he handed me a slip of paper with his address and phone number.

"See you at 7:00," he said.

Numb and immobile, I managed to stutter my thanks. Before I left the store, I reached out to shake his hand. He gazed deeply into my eyes and extended his hand. Our hands touched. Although brief, the warmth of his hands and immediate chemistry between us stirred my pent-up desires. Shaking and trembling, I slowly walked to my car, my palms sweaty.

The minutes crawled by over the next twenty-four hours until 7:00 p.m. To say I was tense would grossly understate. I had longed for affection from another man for so long, I just knew something intimate was about to happen. The signs were there: his deep gaze, his tender handshake.

Upon my arrival, he met me at his door and asked me to come in. As I entered, he came closer to me and offered a hug. As we hugged, I was captivated. Hungry for a man's touch, I hung on to him for several more seconds.

The attraction was magnetic. I pulled away ever so slightly to gaze into his eyes, and our lips met with a kiss both passionate and long.

"M, I'm sorry," I said.

"Don't talk," he hushed me.

Over the next hour, we made passionate love, exhilarating as we explored every inch of each other's body. Finally, our sexual appetites were exhausted.

We talked at great length before I got dressed and headed for the door. We talked about religion, about being gay, about different topics.

I assured him of my gratitude for inviting me over. Knowing this was my first sexual encounter in many years, he was kind and understanding. He told me if I ever needed to chat again, to let him know, but somehow, I realized this was a one-time encounter. I hugged him and left.

On my drive home, I felt 1001 emotions. Thoughts multiplied about the acts I had just committed. *What have I done?* I repeated this over and over in my tortured mind.

When I arrived at my apartment, I was almost a basket-case. I fell to my knees and begged God's forgiveness for such backsliding. "Lord, have mercy on me," I prayed as I wept.

After I fell into the loving arms of my God that night, I awoke the next morning in a state of utter confusion. For eight years I had lived a celibate life, no intimacy with another man, not even a kiss, and now, look at what I had done! At this point, a scab of disappointment began to form over my heart towards my God. Though the disappointment would be short-lived, it did teach me a valuable lesson in grace.

To add insult to injury, the friend of mine whose sister was married to Tom's brother confronted me, saying that she knew about the liaison between Tom and me. I was stunned. No privacy! Instantly, I felt condemnation deepen.

"How did you find out?" I asked.

"It's not important," she responded.

"I'm sorry you had to find out, Kay."

"Don, I love you. This doesn't change anything. You know God forgives."

"I know He does, Kay."

This collapse in judgment in my life in 1991 was just the beginning of the crumbling of my house of cards of faith. I did not know then that God had a plan, His plan, one much higher and greater than I could ever imagine. As we read in *Isaiah 55*:8, "'For my thoughts are not your thoughts, neither are your ways my ways,' saith the Lord."

In the days and years that followed this collapse of my judgment, I came to know a God of great grace and mercy, a God of compassion, and a God Who loves us despite our weaknesses and disappointments. In his compassionate song, "You'll See A Man," singer/songwriter Ed Kerr writes, "In days gone by, you felt so sure. Now dreams of joy and peace fade in memories. Once you hungered for His word, he seemed so near, now the distance seems to grow with every heart-beat. Somehow you feel you've gone too far, no reason to try. But He's with you where you are. You'll see a man... He knows your weakness disappoints you. He knows we're vessels made of clay. But He'll never leave, let your heart believe. You're secure, safe in His hands. You'll see a man acquainted with your sorrows. You'll see His eyes sharing in your tears. You'll see His arms never lost their hold on you. Lift your eyes, you'll see the Lord."

A LONG-LOST HEART WITHIN REACH

I walked Myrtle Beach alone one night in 1993, as the waves crashed against the shore. I listened to Elton John's latest single, "The One," on my Walkman, with the warm sea breeze at my back and the cry of seagulls above my head when a line from the song gripped my heart as I gazed out into the darkness of the ocean. These words written by Bernie Taupin and Elton John penetrated me,

For each man in his time is Cain,

Until he walks along the beach,

And sees his future in the water,

A long-lost heart within his reach.

My heart had been lost for so long, no romance, only teachings full of how wrong my same-sex attraction was. Full of faith in Christ, I was muddled by all the dogma and insecurities of my sexual orientation. This battle in my mind had drained all the joy from my life. Instead of a life where "the joy of the Lord was my strength," any joy I had received became degraded by my conflicted mind.

Suddenly, a glimmer appeared, as if a ship at sea had emitted a bright light. Hope arose in my soul.

An acute desire for intimacy and love awakened in me that night on the beach. To live without this is almost a living death. But once one gets a taste of love's consuming qualities, one begins to live, one's life is renewed. He at once envisions a future with hope within his grasp.

It has been over twenty-five years now since that dark night when I walked the shores of Myrtle Beach, but in my memory, the feeling is as fresh as if it had just happened.

There is a tranquility and comfort when I'm at the ocean. I will never forget the weekend after we buried my precious mother, Anna Belle. She had given me a crystal many years before and had told me, "Someday when I am gone, look in the rainbows that the crystal makes, and I'll be in the rainbows."

The Saturday after I returned to Orlando, after we had buried Mom, I was driving east on the 408 in Orlando. As I turned to go south, the sun shined on the crystal Mom had given me years before, and rainbows filled my car. Then I knew Mom would always be with me. I can feel her with me all the time.

Mom loved the ocean, and so do I. The ocean gives me solace. The ocean reminds me of how majestic and awesome our God is.

The writers of the song sung by Elton John won't know how much their song spoke to me on that night at Myrtle Beach, but I do know: the future I saw in the water that night, is the future I am in now.

RECKLESS ABANDON

The term "reckless abandon" suggests doing something without regard for the consequences. During the mid-1990s residing in Huntington, West Virginia, I lived my life in a chronic state of reckless abandon, my emotions tossed about by feelings of desperation, loneliness, emptiness, and frustration. In a disillusioned state of faith, I whiled away the night hours cruising a part of Huntington known in the gay community so I could connect with other men.

In the daytime, Harris Riverfront Park in Huntington with its picturesque backdrop of the Ohio River and the downtown skyline, shined as a bustling harbor for joggers, picnic tables for local businesses and a marina to house boating enthusiasts. But at night, the location became a desolate spot notorious for cruising for sex.

On an ordinary night, you would find scores of cars, trucks, even motorcyclists driving along the boulevard, a three-block radius of the park, with the gleam of headlights in both directions. Intermittently you would see the tap of brake lights, indicating a passerby's interest. As you enter into the park from the boulevard, you would cross a railroad track. Once over the tracks you would be inside Harris Riverfront Park, a riverfront made more private by the floodwalls protecting the city in the event of the Ohio River's flooding.

Under the canopy of the night sky, urged on by a lethargic and listless indifference for life itself, I allowed my disappointments with life and most importantly, my faith, to compel me into this desperate state of loneliness, emptiness and reckless abandon.

Weary of the internal struggle of a tortured mind pulling my spirit down, I felt enveloped in a black cloak, hedged in by the dread of a day-to-day existence with my life on a road to nowhere. In an effort to endure such a meaningless existence, I sought out the elusive prince I had always dreamed of. Blinded to the dangers of such a promiscuous pathway, though I tried to connect with many men, sex with these strangers failed to fill the hollowness of my wayward heart.

Now, as I look back on this chapter of waywardness, I am thankful that I never contracted a sexually transmitted disease. Somehow, I crawled out of the reckless abandon episode in my life. And although there would be other dangers awaiting me down the road, to this day, I am confident of God's providence and mercy during one of the lowest points of my life.

A FINAL ATTEMPT AT HETEROSEXUALITY

In my desperate attempt to crawl out of that rabbit hole I had dug for myself in the mid-to-late 1990s, I was hungry for the redeeming touch of the Lord. After I visited a few churches in the Huntington area, I decided to give Jefferson Avenue Church of God one last try.

The church prided itself on welcoming home the backslider. A back-slider being a Christian who falls back into sin, a relapse into bad, sinful habits.

As I began to attend the church where I felt so at home, M, an ex-girlfriend who knew all too well the struggles I had faced with the same sex, welcomed me back with open arms.

It was also during this time that her dad passed away, a death that affected her deeply. Not long after that, the trailer where she and her mom lived burned. A devastating event for her and her mom. These events brought M and me closer. Sometimes compassion for someone can be confused with love. Unfortunately, I believe this is what happened to M and myself.

During the horrible event of the trailer's burning, M's mom suffered a debilitating stroke and was hospitalized for several weeks. This caused substantial bonding between M and me.

As M's mother began to heal and they found a new place to live, M and I had become quite close. I believe it was during this period where I allowed compassion and empathy to cloud my judgment. I was to the point where I would have done anything to please God.

Through some close friends at the church, I allowed the seed of thought to be planted in my heart that perhaps M was the perfect wife for me. She seemed to bring out the best in me; she encouraged me in the Lord. M was adamantly opposed to homosexuality, so I took this as a good thing. Not realizing at the time that burying these feelings for the same sex would someday come back to haunt me.

CRACKS IN THE WALL AGAINST TEMPTATION

Autumn 1994

State Route 10 between Huntington, WV, and Logan, WV, with its sharp hairpin curves, would frustrate the best NASCAR racer.

On an autumn morning in 1994, M and her mother, G, and I made the long drive to Logan for G's sister's birthday party. I was driving M's Oldsmobile Cutlass Supreme. Frequently over the hour and a half drive, M would casually caress my hand as she sat beside me in the front seat. Did I experience feelings of love and excitement when she did this? No. On the contrary, I often rebuffed her romantic gestures.

M was a beautiful woman, standing about 5'4", having a medium build with shoulder-length light brown hair, often dressed in colored skirts and flats. She was ten years my senior. Her soft complexion and hazel eyes added to her beauty.

Well aware of my homosexuality, all she would ever say to me about the subject was that I needed to be "delivered." I could talk to her until I was blue in the face about my being attracted to the same sex, and I would always get the same tyrannical response, "It's of the Devil," she would say.

I never felt a natural attraction to M that I felt towards some men, but I'd convinced myself I needed her in my life. Strangely, she'd become the wall of temptation and fortitude I needed to counterattack my temptations toward men. On this particular trip together, I was to face one of the fiercest battles of my life.

Arriving in Logan at G's sister R's house, we met a multitude of relatives wholly unfamiliar to me. We entered through the back door and proceeded into R's large kitchen, and suddenly I was taken aback: There he stood, one of the most handsome guys I'd ever laid eyes on, tall, trimmed beard and mustache, dark brown hair and beautiful brown eyes. He reached out to shake my hand as we were introduced. I was so captivated I could barely speak.

A little later, I learned his name was T, M's first cousin. For the remainder of the day, no matter how hard I tried to stay calm and dote on M, in my mind flashed the images of this ruggedly handsome man, with his clean-cut beard, open shirt, and hairy chest.

The laws of attraction are mysterious. We don't always get to choose to whom we're attracted. I'd always been attracted to hairy-chested men, and T fit that mold completely. Fortunately, T and M both were oblivious to the battle raging inside me, my private hell on that day.

M had been able to toss certain of my magazines in the garbage to fend off my temptations, but this crack in the wall against temptation at her aunt R's house on that autumn day was a harbinger of things to come.

It wasn't long after this that I convinced myself that I should ask M to marry me. One evening as she and I ate dinner at Olive Garden, I got down on one knee and asked her if she would marry me. She said yes.

By this time, it was late 2000. After much discussion, M and I chose May 19, 2001, as our wedding date.

In the months leading up to the wedding, one incident sticks out in my mind. We had come to my apartment after church one night, and as had often been the case, my tabby cat, Belle, jumped up on my lap, and I began petting her. For some reason, this annoyed M, and she snapped, "You're supposed to pay attention to me."

How I wish I had paid more attention to detail this evening. Possibly I might have saved myself a lot of grief. But my heart was too focused on what I perceived to be God's will, and doing His will mattered most to me.

PART IV
MARRIAGE AND DIVORCE (2001)

CHAPTER 10

MARRIAGE, MY BIG MISTAKE?

WEDDING DAY (19 MAY 2001)

At three minutes before seven on that 19th day of May in 2001, my eyelids burst open, the restless night finally over. As anxious thoughts raced through my mind, I lay paralyzed with dread, aware of the day's impending event. I whispered a prayer to God for peace.

A wedding should be one of the happiest moments in a person's life, yet I was anything but happy on this climactic morning. I clung to a stubborn faith that it was God's will to marry this woman, half convinced that the marriage would solidify a permanent change in my sexual orientation.

By Saturday afternoon, the sanctuary of the Jefferson Avenue Church of God in Huntington, WV, had been transformed into one of solemnity and celebration. The bridal canopy dazzled, adorned with floral arrangements of coral garden roses and peonies. An array of spring flowers decorated the first five rows down from the altar.

Soft wedding music played in the background. As the sunlight's radiant beams illuminated the stained-glass windows, I sighed. With each passing moment, the muscles in my shoulders tightened. My feet immovable, I pondered the gravity of the moment as terror gripped my heart. I once again muttered a prayer, "Lord, help me to do this."

Alone in an adjacent room off the sanctuary, I was a nervous wreck. Although the best man, my brother Stan, was near, I had resolved to do this alone. This mountain of doubt, to be conquered, had to be conquered through my own faith and trust in God.

I had long imagined my wedding ceremony to be a time of great excitement and celebration, not a time of dread and uncertainty. Striving to personify a free spirit, I was on a collision course with my emotions. Still, I clung to my faith, forcing my mind to rationalize such promises from God's Word as, "He that findeth a wife, findeth a good thing. [Proverbs 18:22]

Despite reassurance from scripture, negative thoughts assailed me. *Will I fail at this marriage, and make a fool of myself? What are my friends and family thinking, especially those who know I've struggled with same-sex attractions? Will I be made a laughingstock? What persuades me to think I can live a heterosexual lifestyle?* My mind was a battlefield.

Until that day, I felt strong emotionally. Then, suddenly, defenseless against the barrage of self-doubt and fear of failure, I began to question myself, *Is it common to question the state of your emotions on one's wedding day? Or was it just pre-wedding jitters?*

I was a man committed to pleasing God, yet without warning, my faith was under attack. I felt what faith I did have seep from my body. I desired to please God, but I was perplexed at this unexpected onslaught.

In a secluded room off the sanctuary, my brother Stan and I began to don our black tuxedos. He did his best to encourage me, but as minutes passed, my restlessness tightened its grip. My hands were sweaty;

my heart beat faster. I was a nervous wreck.

Stan, aware of my restlessness, offered a heartfelt prayer, "Lord, let Your peace fall upon Don."

In retrospect, this wasn't just a wedding but also a culmination of my faith. Determined to please God, I didn't want it to be said of me that I didn't trust God. If I failed, it would be colossal. I had no choice but to triumph over my fears.

All my life, I'd regarded marriage as a solemn act. Now, minutes before the ceremony, I came face-to-face with my own unworthiness to be part of such a sacred ceremony. Could I be faithful to a woman? Wasn't God's standard for holy matrimony established for heterosexuals? Would I magically become attracted to M from this day forward? Doubt assailed me.

A half-hour before the ceremony, I began to hear the muffled voices of guests as they entered the sanctuary. My belly full of butterflies, I began to shake all over. Fearful thoughts, such as *I can't do this*, raced through my mind. For a few seconds, I even fought the urge to run. Desperately, trying to ignore my tormented psyche, I again whispered a soft prayer for strength and obedience to my God.

My faith had sustained me through many difficult trials in my life. I prayed for it not to fail me now. As I clung to this faith, I felt as if I would drown. Desperately, I cried out, "Lord, help me!"

A friend of mine frantically tipped me off that M hadn't yet shown up to the church. Oddly, I was relieved. Had she come to her senses and realized the marriage was a mistake? However, within minutes, I was told she had arrived. With this bit of news, the jitters returned…with a vengeance.

No matter how hard I had aspired to be a heterosexual, competent to marry a woman, deep inside I knew I was a gay man. I had fasted, prayed for deliverance, sought help through ex-gay ministries, all to no avail.

For years, I had tried to see myself through the mirror of God's Word as a new creature in Christ, "old things are passed away, behold, all things become new." I'd been taught repeatedly that as a new creature in Christ, I was not a homosexual. That this was a lie from the Devil. Because of this teaching, I tried desperately to convince myself I was not gay. Each morning, I prayed a warfare prayer, applying God's armor as described in the *New Testament* book of *Ephesians*, chapter six, reinforcing through prayer the teachings that I was this new creature in Christ. To call myself a gay man was a lie straight out of Hell. So, I had been taught.

Had I allowed the influence of the Pentecostal church to persuade me to take this leap into marriage? After years of holiness teaching that homosexuality was a damning sin, had I conditioned my mind to believe that I wasn't gay, despite what my heart told me? Now, at a crossroads, my allegiance to these teachings faltered.

The stage was set for the wedding ceremony. My best man, Stan, Pastor L, and I walked soberly into the sanctuary. Soft music played. The large number of guests in attendance startled me. As I glanced over the crowd, my body pulsated.

We took our places at the front of the sanctuary. The sublime *Wedding March* began. What fear I felt lifted like a vapor. The guests stood; the bridal procession entered from the back of the church. The flower girls, bridesmaid, and matron of honor moved toward the front of the sanctuary. Next came the triumphant entry of the bride. The *Wedding March* escalated to a magnificent crescendo and every eye focused on M. Stunning in her white lace gown, she was radiant.

For a few brief seconds, my insecurities melted away. My emotions overflowed; my eyes moistened. Elated at the prospect of M becoming my wife, I held my head high. As she drew near, I took my place beside her. Through her veil, I saw the glow of her countenance.

The minister began the invocation, as a hush fell over the crowd. When Pastor L introduced M and me to the audience and told of the purpose of the gathering, I beamed from ear to ear. When I caught a glimpse of M so beautiful in her white gown, I was humbled she would want me as her husband.

The moment drew near for M and me to take our vows. The brevity of the procedure sobered me. I sighed and courageously entered into the marriage contract. After reciting our vows and exchanging wedding bands, we were declared by Pastor Lee as husband and wife.

I lifted M's veil and gave her a long kiss, then took her hand as we walked down the aisle toward the back of the sanctuary and on to the reception in the basement.

The guests numbered about one hundred fifty. In the receiving line of the reception, I put on a brave face, smiling and thanking people for coming. M glowed, no hint of the storm churning deep in my heart.

From that day forward, our lives would never be the same. Soon, cracks in the seemingly perfect union began to show.

The first hint of trouble arose when my sister came up to me on the parking lot of the church right after the reception and said ever so bluntly, "You're not happy, are you?" She knew her brother too well. I could not fool her.

I feigned a smile.

Ominous signs of an imminent marital downfall began when M and I stopped by my apartment to change clothes. As we stood in the kitchen, my fallen countenance revealed to her something was amiss.

"What's wrong, Don?" she asked, alarmed.

A forlorn expression engulfed my once-cheerful countenance. I blurted out, "This marriage was a mistake, M."

I mumbled next that I felt trapped.

She responded with rage, "It's the Devil, Don."

I was repulsed by this criticism, infuriated by a response I'd heard time and time again from her.

Before I could rebuke her, there was a knock at the door. The Associate Pastor from our church had come by to drop off pictures he'd taken at the wedding. While he was there, I put on a brave face.

On the tip of my tongue were the words, "I've made a mistake," but the words were never spoken.

After he left, M persuaded me that we were doing God's will. She took my hand ever so gently and asked the Lord to strengthen me with courage. For a brief respite, I felt lighter.

I continued to cling to my faith that I had pleased God in this marriage, but my faith began to falter. I was having a hard time convincing myself that I had done the right thing. I felt as though I walked in a fog. My feelings were afire.

M did her best to try and console me by touching and hugging me, but I pulled away each time, making her even angrier by the moment, convincing her the more I was allowing the Devil to control me.

As I drove us to Charleston, WV, for our first night as a married couple, words were sparse during the hour-long drive. Driving east on Interstate 64 towards Charleston, we listened to a Christian CD. One of the songs was about believing God amid doubt. M immediately reminded me that the Devil was lying to me. I bought into her comfort, and once again began to hope that this marriage could work.

Once we had checked into our hotel for the night, I endured a quiet dinner with my new wife. Few words were spoken. With my feelings still on edge and very raw, we returned to the hotel room. After she showered, she attempted to change the mood, but I became more distant.

M, perturbed, chided, "Don, snap out of it."

I then became more perplexed than I had been earlier. As M attempted to display affection, I pulled away, shunning her advances, putting her almost in tears, although I sensed it was anger more than sadness she felt.

Instead of trying to make amends on our wedding night, I told her I was going to sleep on the couch. Honestly, I didn't want her touching me. I kept thinking to myself, *how did I get myself into this mess?* For the rest of the night, few words were spoken.

SECOND DAY OF THE HONEYMOON

After my first night as an unconsummated married man, I awoke to the darkness of the hotel room at the Hampton Inn, my back aching from a sleepless night on the sofa. M, asleep on the bed just a few feet away, was acutely aware that our hearts were miles apart.

When she awoke, our greetings were shallow, devoid of any romantic gestures expected of newlyweds.

"We need to pray, Don," M said, breaking the silence. Moved by a sudden twinge of compassion, I agreed. As I knelt beside her and after she tenderly placed her hand over mine, she softly began to pray, asking the Lord to help us fight the powers of darkness she believed were trying to tear us apart.

We ate a light breakfast at the hotel, then embarked on our second day's journey as husband and wife. Although we had discussed Niagara Falls as a honeymoon destination, the dramatic events of the previous night had altered my direction. I now wanted to hurry back to Huntington for an annulment.

Perhaps as an answer to the prayer she had just prayed, I consented to her wish for us to attend a worship service on this Sabbath day. Despite all the turmoil up to this point in our short marriage, I still longed to please God and do His will, no matter the cost. I hoped that I could be what God, and M, wanted me to be.

Seeking a church service to attend, we chose a church west of Charleston, WV, in Teays Valley. We drove west on Interstate 64, the luscious green hillsides of the West Virginia landscape sprawled before us. It dawned on me that there had never been a time in my life with so much at stake. Even so, I felt refreshed as I breathed in the mountain air and heard the sounds of nature from the nearby fields.

We arrived at the church just a few minutes before the 11:00 a.m. service began. Introducing ourselves, M mentioned to one of the staff that we were newlyweds. How I wished she hadn't! Now I had to wear a smile on my face under the pretense I was the happy groom. We took a seat on a bench toward the back of the church.

The service began with an opening prayer by the Pastor and a call to worship, and then we were introduced to the congregation as newlyweds. The congregation erupted in applause. At once, my heart sunk. Fear again raced through my body, and I felt the nuptial noose tighten.

M was a heterosexual woman, expecting to be treated as such. I, on the other hand, was a homosexual, one half-convinced of the need for carrying out the demands of a heterosexual relationship. Confused and bewildered at times, I continued to put my confidence in God to work His will in my life.

Despite my sudden urge to bolt out of the church, I remained seated on the bench beside my new wife. It took all the courage I could muster, but I endured the remainder of the service.

Perhaps something in the sermon that morning had inspired me to further trust God in the marriage: a renewed vigor to do God's will, which meant to me that I would do my best to be truly married to my wife, was suddenly awakened. The fervor I felt an hour earlier to return to Huntington for an annulment had melted away.

SECOND NIGHT, AN INCOMPLETE UNION

As night fell upon M and me on our second evening as husband and wife, all I could think about was the avoidance of consummating our marriage. There I was, a forty-year-old gay man, a virgin, who had never been sexually attracted to women. Although I had dated girls in my early teens and in junior high school, I never had a natural attraction to a woman as I had to a man.

In the small town of Ashtabula, Ohio, that Sunday evening, we checked in to an elegant hotel for the night. As the blushing bride, M no doubt disclosed we were newlyweds: we were given a special price on a suite at the hotel.

M and I returned to the suite after a quiet dinner in the restaurant of the hotel. The suite was a spacious accommodation, with a cheerful décor of bright colors and a soothing upbeat atmosphere. It had a large kitchen, a queen-size bed, a huge bathroom, and a modern television--necessary amenities to make newlyweds feel at home.

The mood was set for a night of passionate lovemaking. For me, however, it was a moment I dreaded. A natural inclination to make love to a woman wasn't there. Just how long would I be able to wear a disguise, the pretense that I was your average virile heterosexual male ready to pounce on this woman and make love to her?

M excused herself to take a shower. In the meantime, sensing intimate moments forthcoming, I changed into more appropriate attire, a pair of boxer shorts. Then it happened! As I was lying in bed, M boldly strolled out of the bathroom naked, her breasts exposed to me for the first time. They were huge, bouncing up and down. I might have said, "Wow!"

She saw me lying there, and her hands were suddenly all over me. She started kissing my neck, and she asked me to kiss her. Caught up in the moment, I began to kiss her neck.

Something happened that surprised me, as we were kissing. I became aroused with a full-blown erection. Seeing my erect penis, M's eyes got big and a lustful expression graced her face. Probably she had never seen an erection before. I began to blush.

The stage was set for my first sexual encounter with a woman. After several minutes of lovemaking, our bodies entangled, kissing each other all over, exploring each other's body, the decisive moment came to enter her. As we attempted to come together, one flesh to couple to another, we hit a brick wall. Like the proverbial virgin on his wedding night, I couldn't find the right opening.

Somewhat perplexed as to what to do next, M tried to guide me to enter her, but neither of us knew quite what to do. After several minutes, frustrated, I stopped abruptly. "I can't do this," I said. Sensing my frustration, she fell back into the bed.

We lay for several minutes in that queen-size bed. I felt like I had floundered in my attempt at making love with my new wife. Although I was partly relieved not to have to complete the act, the pressure of being a married man who had not yet consummated his marriage troubled me.

Only time would tell if we would make a second attempt at making love.

DIRE STRAITS IN NIAGARA FALLS

The journey for M and me in our brief marriage had been turbulent. Despite each setback, I had high hopes the rocky road we'd traveled would evolve into a joyous celebration of our union.

Here I was, under the canopy of blue skies, bathed with sunshine, at one of the world's most popular landmarks, Niagara Falls, with my new bride of fewer than three days, and I didn't want to be here.

Upon arrival, we had exhausted ourselves for over an hour in a quest for a hotel spotless enough to meet M's high standards for cleanliness. She, a former health inspector, demanded the room be immaculate, especially the bathroom. After overly fastidious inspections of several hotel rooms, I grew agitated.

M, conscious of my frustration, resented my impatience. "I won't stay in a room that is not clean, and especially if there is mold anywhere in the bathroom," she announced.

Once we had found an acceptable room, we were on the brink of an argument. "I'm sorry," I said, instead.

After we had settled in the room, the tension between us had greatly diminished. We decided to stroll around the vicinity of the hotel to find a nice restaurant in which to have dinner.

We enjoyed a quiet dinner at a quaint restaurant near the falls, and we walked through an arcade on our way back to the room. A failed attempt to hold my hand as we walked caused her to launch into a tirade about my lack of affection toward her.

M had no trouble fanning the flames in an argument. As this argument intensified, I grew angrier because each time she complained about my lack of intimacy toward her, the accusation always came back around to how I was allowing demonic influences to control me.

By the time we reached our hotel room, I was fuming. As so many times before, her rhetoric not merely annoyed me, it made me feel enough was enough. When she perceived how mad I had gotten, she became furious herself, and she stormed out of the hotel room.

Alone in the hotel room, I felt a sense of relief. Glad that I didn't have her breathing down my neck, I stretched out on the bed and tried to rest. I fell asleep, lost track of time, and awoke to find the hotel room was dark. M had probably been gone for about an hour. Abruptly, the hotel room door flew open. She began an outburst about how she had gotten lost. In tears, she hurled the accusations against me: it was my fault she had gotten lost and my lack of concern for her welfare called into question how I could claim to love her.

The argument escalated. We were almost shouting. To end the ruckus, M suggested we call my sister-in-law, Gayle. I calmed down and agreed to call Gayle at her home in West Virginia.

M and I had the utmost respect for Gayle. We all three attended the same church. After a lengthy conversation with Gayle, informing her of what had transpired between M and me since the wedding, Gayle began to reprimand me. She, too, went on angrily about how I'm in spiritual warfare, maintaining that the Devil was trying to destroy what the Lord was attempting to build between M and me.

In my continuing effort to please God, I allowed Gayle to pray with me over the phone. M, listening to our conversation, joined in on the prayer, putting her arms around me as Gayle prayed. I did feel a sense of relief from her prayer, but at the same time, doubts lingered as to how long I could continue this fierce conflict between the two of us.

After we had prayed and the conversation had ended, I apologized to M for the earlier argument, blaming myself for her getting lost. After this, we went to bed and shared a restful night, one with no further attempt to make love.

POINT OF NO RETURN

The warmth of the morning sun failed to loosen the grip on my cold heart, as M and I faced an uncertain future in a loveless marriage.

Each new day had brought us a brief reprieve from eruptions threatening to undermine our union. Our wedding had been less than a week prior, and we were heading home from our "honeymoon."

One such reprieve occurred when I allowed my sister-in-law, Gayle, to pray with me. In her prayer, as she pleaded with the Lord to fortify my resistance to what she felt was demonic forces against me, I felt for one shining moment renewed in the sacred vows I had made to M.

The next morning, however, the brief respite from the turmoil which had plagued my emotions came back with a vengeance. My feelings toward M had become as cold as the waters which flowed over Niagara Falls itself. Suddenly, like waking from a nightmare, I shuddered in disbelief about the mess I had made of my life.

As I drove us back toward West Virginia, the shifting landscape of the northern Ohio countryside stretched out before us. For miles, the level terrain, dotted with silos and rich farmland, began to take on a more rugged, Appalachian tone. By the time we had entered West Virginia, the view had become a rural country scene of farmhouses and livestock. We were shrouded in hills and deep valleys. It suddenly dawned on me: my life had become like this inconstant landscape, fickle and unstable. It seemed there was little I could do about it.

M had brandished random outbursts of aggressive behavior from time to time. In the ten years we had dated before our wedding, I experienced such contentious behavior only a handful of times.

As long as she received attention, M exhibited love and affection. However, when something didn't go her way or she failed to get the attention she wanted, her anger flared, and she became possessive.

The silence of our drive was broken when M pleaded, "Don, please talk to me. Don't shut me out. With the Lord's help, we can make this marriage work."

"What if we can't, M?"

Possibly angered by my indifference, she escalated, "Stop it, Don! You're listening to the Devil."

I thought she was going to slap me. As she raised her hand, I shouted, "M, I'm driving! Get ahold of yourself!"

Unfazed, she continued, "The Lord is in this marriage, Don. If it fails, it's because you allowed the Devil to destroy it."

A prolonged silence filled the air.

Then, ever so softly, she whispered, "I'm sorry, Don," and with her voice trembling she added, "I love you. You have to want this marriage to work."

"I am doing my best, M," I said hesitantly, trying to convince her, more than myself, for I had already felt the impending demise of this short marriage deep in my heart.

I mustered all the cheerfulness I could for the remainder of the drive back to Huntington. My future looked bleak. Hanging by a thread to what little bit of faith I had, I felt my determination to please God in the marriage waning. Under the weight of my guilt for not pleasing God in this marriage, I also felt a seed of dread growing deep in my heart as the sense of failure loomed.

Back in Huntington with its familiar cobblestone streets and memories of a happier time, I longed to erase the profound dread I felt. As I drove M and me straight to the apartment we would share with M's mom, Lee, so we could unpack, I felt apprehensive to be alone with M. I was not in the mood for any of her romantic overtures, nor did I want another heated confrontation between us because of my lack of affection toward her. All I wanted was to be alone.

The apartment was empty. M's mother, L, had not returned from staying with her sister while we were away on our honeymoon.

L, a humble, short, grandmotherly type in her late 70s, with the deepest blue eyes and white, wavy hair, a woman of strong faith, had always been kind to me. I can picture her beautiful smile to this day.

She and M had a strong mother/daughter bond. Lee knew I had struggled with homosexuality, and perhaps this is why she had never put her stamp of approval on our getting married. Although she never said it, I sensed she never trusted me.

At the apartment, I clung to what little hope I had things would get better between M and me, although the last rays of hope of this dying relationship were fading rapidly.

After we unloaded the car and were inside the apartment, we may have prayed, asking the Lord to strengthen us. I don't remember. Uneasiness permeated my being.

The roller coaster of emotions wearied me. With each new day, I became increasingly edgy, as I sunk deeper into despair. M and I argued constantly. I displayed little or no affection toward her. When she would try to kiss me or show any affection to me, I would pull away, only angering her more.

By my continual rejection of her advances, the great gulf between us became more obvious. Sadly, M hadn't realized I had already come to the point of no return in this short marriage.

When M's mother came home late that evening, I did my best to appear glad to see her. After some small talk and sharing some brighter moments of our honeymoon, I excused myself and went into the bedroom M and I would share, so I could be alone, and M and her mother could talk. I offered up what must have been brief prayers, climbed in bed, and drifted into a restless sleep. I awoke during the night, finding to my surprise that M had never come to bed. I figured she must have decided to sleep with her mother. Oddly, I felt relieved.

I awoke the next morning with M nudging me, "Don, you need to get up. We need to talk." Sitting on the edge of the bed, M lit into me. "Why are you being so hateful to me. You never want to kiss me or hug me. What is wrong with you, Don? You are not the man I thought you were."

I tried to explain to her the dilemma I was in, how miserable I felt, all to no avail. For several minutes she continued to scold me for the excuses I made for my behavior.

After a few minutes of silence, she hugged me, and we embraced. "I'm sorry, Don. I can't take much more of being treated like a stranger. I am your wife, whether you want to treat me like it or not."

After a few minutes, we both knelt beside the bed, and we prayed, "Lord, we need You to strengthen us. We desperately need Your help."

After breakfast, we left to go get my things from my old apartment. We rented a U-Haul and drove to the apartment to pack up everything, M and I then faced the chore of renting a storage building to put what belongings of mine that wouldn't fit into the small apartment we'd share with her mother.

The tension once again began to build. It had been a long day. Our pressure-cooker relationship was ready to blow. We began shouting at one another over trivia: the cost of the storage building; how I needed to watch my spending; we even argued about my cat, Belle. M's mother didn't like cats. She only went along with having Belle to appease me.

It was now Friday evening. M and I had worn ourselves out in putting what belongings of mine wouldn't fit into the apartment in a storage building. Now, back at my "new home" with M and her mother, I tried to put on a happy face, but in reality, I was dying inside.

THE LAST WEEKEND

The moments crept by that final weekend as the great gulf between M and I widened. The final blow came Sunday morning as we visited the church where we had married a little over a week before.

If it had been up to me, I would have sneaked into the sanctuary through the back, sat on one of the last pews, and not made a peep. But no, M wanted a more dignified entrance. She chose for us to walk in, hand in hand, sit with her family and a few friends directly in the middle of the pews, conspicuously projecting us as happy newlyweds to the congregation.

As we sat there, packed liked sardines in the crowded pew, I felt as if all eyes were focused on me, judging my every move. Surely it wasn't M they watched. It was me. The guy so many had come to know as a supposed overcomer of homosexuality. They had observed me model the supposed ex-gay over the years. Striving to adhere to their strict doctrine of anti-gay teachings, all the while browbeating myself into almost hysteria. It was now time for me to shine. To glorify God by allowing His grace to work a great miracle in my life. No doubt, many wondered had I succeeded in pulling off this feat? Further proving to a strict, anti-gay, religious sect that one can become ex-gay. Had I completely been delivered from the sin so many perceived as the blackest of sins, even to the point of living a heterosexual life with a woman?

Within minutes, as I sat there hemmed in next to the woman who was legally my wife, tormenting accusations flooded my mind. As they intertwined with the failures I felt from this past week, a feeling of despair overwhelmed me.

Within a congregation where I had once felt comfortable and accepted, I now felt like an enemy. It was as if they were reading my thoughts and feelings. I knew too well the shaky ground M I now walked on. It wouldn't be long before many of our friends and family would read the signs that things weren't as they appeared in our storybook marriage.

As I sat there and the pressure within mounted, suddenly, the pastor announced M and I were in attendance. As soon as the words fell from his lips, everyone turned and looked at us. My heart sank.

As M and I stood, the crowd of nearly 200 people cheered. For any other couple, this would be a beautiful moment. But for me, it was pure torture. I didn't love this woman standing next to me. I hid behind a façade of deception. In the embarrassment of the moment, my legs wobbled. Humiliation engulfed me like a dark cloud. The few minutes we stood seemed an eternity.

In that instant, more than at any other time, I knew the marriage was over. As a deep sense of hopelessness engulfed me, I knew I could no longer endure wearing this mask I had worn for so long. I could no longer lie to myself, to M, and most importantly, to God. Somehow, I had to come clean. I had to find a way to rid myself of the pressure now too great to bear. As the sensation of being trapped began to overpower me, and before panic had its full effect, I would need to find a way to endure the remainder of the service, acting as if everything between M and me was okay.

The minutes ticked by ever so slowly for the remainder of the service. Raw, anxious feelings made my skin crawl. I could barely endure them. It took every ounce of strength I had to keep my composure.

By the time the service ended, I was sitting on pins and needles. I had to get out of the church before panic overtook me. At my beckoning, M followed me out of the church. When she asked why I was in such a hurry, I came up with the excuse that I wasn't feeling well.

In truth, I wasn't feeling well. Just what malady affected me, she would find out soon enough.

THE DEPARTURE

Few words were spoken after M and I left church that Sunday afternoon. As I retreated inwardly to cope with the paralyzing sense of the world caving in on me, the silence between us carried over into that night.

I tossed and turned in an empty bed with fitful rages of restlessness, and sometime during the night, I made a pivotal decision that would alter the rest of my life.

I awoke before dawn Monday morning, and though the storm raged inside me, a deep, settled peace soothed my troubled mind. When M awoke, few words were spoken. The tension remained thick, yet no hint did I give of the decisive act I planned.

As the minutes crept closer for me to leave for work, I briefly cradled my tabby, Belle, in my arms. As I stroked her, I remembered the instance when M had snapped at me for petting her. Upon memory of this, I looked M in the eye as I put Belle down and said one final good-bye as I walked out the door.

Outside the door, I sighed for a few seconds, then started walking toward my car. I couldn't get there fast enough. Once inside my car, a peace I hadn't felt for weeks enveloped me. As I drove away from the apartment, I glanced back one more time through the rear-view mirror, thinking to myself, I will never go back.

I thought no more of M until sometime after lunch when she called me at work.

"Why haven't you called me?" she asked.

"I have nothing left to say," I replied.

As I dodged her interrogation about my lack of love shown toward her, finally I blurted, "M, I won't be back."

In a suspicious voice, almost yelling, she said, "What do you mean, you won't be back? I am your wife. You can't just walk out on me."

Firmly resolved, I reiterated, "M, I am not coming back."

After several seconds, in a disgusted tone, she replied, "I knew you weren't planning to come back. You are listening to the Devil. He will take you straight to Hell, Don."

As silence lingered on the line, I said, "Goodbye, M."

———————◆———————

I had spoken to Mom a few times since the wedding but never a hint of any trouble in paradise. But mothers have a sixth sense about their children. When I finally found enough nerve to go by her house that evening, she nonchalantly asked, "What's wrong?"

"How could you tell something was wrong?" I asked.

In her loving way, she replied, "A mother knows." As she reached out to hug me, I fought back tears.

When I finally spoke, I said, "Mom, this marriage was a mistake. I'm not going back to her."

After a few seconds of silence, she said, "You've always done the right thing."

"No, I haven't, Mom," I said

On that Monday after work, I asked Mom if I could stay with her for a few days until I decided on my course, and she was certainly happy to accommodate me. I was fortunate to have a caring and understanding mother, one who wouldn't judge her son as he trudged through some of the most difficult days in his life. But just because she wouldn't judge me, didn't mean no one else would.

As Mom and I sat around her dining room table on that Monday evening, the first wave of condemnation for the abandonment of my wife would come from my sister-in-law, Gayle. In no uncertain terms, she instructed me to go home to my wife. There were no ifs, ands, or buts about it. These words were coming from a woman who herself had been divorced. The conversation didn't end well. M and Gayle were close friends. M had reached out to Gayle about my decision to walk away from the marriage.

In the day that followed, I asked my former landlord to see if possibly my old apartment was available. To my delight, it was. He told me it was still mine if I wanted it.

BACK IN MY APARTMENT

A valiant commitment to Christ doesn't guarantee one will make the right choices in life. Often, the opposite is true.

Less than two weeks after I had married the woman I felt God intended me to marry, I found myself back in my old apartment, having walked out of the marriage due to irreconcilable differences. I was lucky my former landlord hadn't tried to rent the apartment. He and I were good friends.

Because I was a gay man who couldn't fit into the mold of a heterosexual lifestyle, my faith hadn't failed me, but my resistance to change had, further proving to myself that one couldn't change his sexual orientation.

My one-bedroom apartment felt like home the moment I stepped through the front door into the large living room. A deep-seated peace welcomed me like an old friend. Only one thing was missing, my tabby, Belle, who was still with M. In times past, as soon as I opened the front door, I would hear the bell around Belle's neck rattle as she jumped from my bed onto the hardwood floor and ran to greet me. Now, her absence left a vacuum in my heart.

It might seem heartless to some, and might even anger a few, but I loved Belle more than I could have ever loved M.

I asked my brother Earl to get Belle along with my belongings from M and the storage unit; my life began again to take on a renewed form of happiness and independence.

No longer did I live under the microscope of a wife who constantly nagged me about how much attention I paid or did not pay to her. Now, I could once again live my life as I pleased, not having to answer to anyone.

I didn't question myself as to why I had married this woman, I came to a wiser realization that by making such a colossal mistake, I would begin slowly to come to terms with the acceptance of my being a gay man.

FILING FOR DIVORCE (31 MAY 2001)

When I awoke Friday morning in my one-bedroom apartment, four days after I had walked out of my marriage, the brilliant sunlight of the new day scattered its golden rays across my bed.

I had started this new chapter in my life the moment I walked out on M. Now I braced for the fallout.

I finished my shift as a customer service specialist that afternoon at the nuclear pharmacy, then I got up enough nerve to drive by the Cabell County Court House in Huntington, WV, where I hoped to file for divorce.

I parked my car and walked slowly toward that stately building in the center of downtown Huntington, WV. The afternoon sun shined brightly through the giant oak trees that surrounded this building for legal proceedings. Wholly unaware of my situation, squirrels played in abundance as I walked the narrow sidewalk toward the front steps. Watching them play, I envied their carefree existence. As I drew closer to the steps, I took a deep breath then walked through the glass doors atop the steps.

Once I made it inside the main entrance of the main building, the seriousness of the moment shot through me like a bolt of lightning. More than ever, I envied those squirrels' carefree existence.

Not only had my life unraveled in the last two weeks, but so had M's life. This was her first marriage, and now she was fifty years of age, the event she had waited for all her life was in shambles. Wasn't her anger justified?

Am I the selfish one here? Perhaps I had not tried hard enough to work at this brief marriage and had not fully considered the consequences of a divorce, especially in a holiness church. Or if I had tried as hard as I should have, how was this divorce going to affect my faith? These thoughts flooded my mind before I stepped foot into the circuit clerk's office.

As I bolted through the door, the brightness of the overhead lights must have illuminated my uneasy countenance; in a cautious tone, a circuit clerk asked, "Can I help you?"

"I am here to file for divorce," I said in a strained voice, avoiding eye contact.

"I can help you with that," she replied.

Politely, she asked me, "How long were you married?"

When I told her the brevity of our marriage, her expression changed.

"Have you considered an annulment?"

"No, I haven't," I said.

"You should. It would make the process a lot easier."

Uncertain, I responded, "I'm not sure an annulment is possible."

"Why?" she asked.

After I explained to her that I had been married in a strict holiness church, her next question stunned me a little.

"Did you consummate the marriage?"

Stuttering, I replied, "We, we tried, but no, we didn't."

After a few awkward seconds, gazing at the floor, I asked her, "What's the first step in filing for divorce?"

She explained without hesitation the process of filing the Petition for Divorce in the Circuit Court of Cabell County. Once I had filed the petition, it would then be my responsibility to serve the petition and summons on M.

I filed for divorce at the Cabell County Courthouse, in Huntington. For some reason, an annulment was not possible. Why I don't know. The marriage was never consummated.

At the first hearing with the family law representative, M went into an outburst about how I am a man of God walking out of God's will. She was belligerent. I was humiliated.

After this hearing, I had no verbal communication with M.

Through a process server, I attempted to have the divorce papers served. M refused them. In an almost desperate move, I delivered them to her door. When she didn't answer, I left them. M did not take too kindly to this action. She accused me of harassment.

The divorce hearing took place almost ninety days after we were married, held at the Wayne County Court House because we resided in Wayne County.

A few questions were asked of both of us at the divorce hearing. M was asked is if there were any chance she was pregnant, and she said no. In all honesty, how could she be?

During the formalities at the Court House, we barely looked at each other.

After the divorce decree was signed, I did not say a word to M. I took my copy of the decree and walked out. I hadn't felt as free in a long time.

I did look back at her car as she drove away. In some ways, I felt sorry for her. She did love me. It's sad in that respect.

On my way home from the Wayne County Court House, I went a little out of my way and drove by the house of my friends, T and J, a couple I had known before the marriage. I hadn't talked to them in a long time, having cut ties with my friends who were gay.

A year or so before the marriage, to separate myself from the gay lifestyle, I had cut off all ties to gay friends. I even typed a letter to five gay friends of mine, preaching to them how sinful homosexuality is. This letter didn't go over too well. My friend T was very hurt by this. So much so, that when I showed up in his driveway the day of the divorce, he was caught off guard to see me, having been hurt badly. He still loved me as a friend, but I had hurt him deeply. Later, we began to resume our mutual trust and breach the gap in our friendship.

Over the next month or so, as our friendship began to heal, T and J asked me to house-sit while they were on vacation in Washington, D.C. On Monday, October 15, 2001, I was surfing at the site gay.com when I noticed a guy in the chat room whose name is Juan. Having been attracted to Latin men, I decided to chat with him. After I wrote "hi" to him, he left the chat room. I worried that he wouldn't come back. After a while, he did come back online. We chatted for about an hour. I gave him my number. He called me and we talked for almost five hours. We met the next day.

PART V
POST-DIVORCE

CHAPTER 11

THE ENCOUNTER

In early October, the hillsides of western West Virginia were a spectacular display of yellow, orange, rustic brown, and vibrant red. Temperatures were warm with an occasional breeze shuffling leaves from the nearest maple trees. I was house-sitting for my friends Tim and John on the outskirts of Huntington, WV, a couple of months after my divorce.

Feeling lonely, I decided to jump on the computer and scan the list of names in the West Virginia room of gay.com, a gay chat room, in hopes of finding romance. Finally, for the first time in years, I was once again free to pursue intimacy with a man. I had been wanting this for such a long time. Before my engagement to M, I had dated men, but I had never felt the kind of freedom I felt now.

On that Monday night, the fifteenth day of October of 2001, I was intrigued to find a guy with a Hispanic name, "Juan," in the chat room. Attracted to Latin men, I thought, *if there's a Latin man in Huntington, I want to meet him.*

As I gathered my courage in anticipation of sending this mysterious man a message, my heart began to beat faster. I fired off a simple "hello," and I held my breath in high hopes that I would get a favorable response. A few seconds later came a message, from Juan, saying hi.

After introducing ourselves, we chatted back and forth for twenty minutes before he abruptly left the room. Fearing I might have said something to offend him, or maybe he wasn't interested, I was disappointed, but decided to hang out a little longer in hopes that he would return. To my delight, after a few minutes, he came back to the chat room. (Most online chat rooms are designed to let the user know when another user exits and returns.)

"I'm glad you came back, Juan. I was afraid I had lost you."

"I had to take care of something. Besides, you can't get rid of me that easily," he quipped. As we continued the conversation from where we left off, we talked for over an hour getting to know each other. We shared stories about our vocations, our families, and the type of guy we were attracted to. After I revealed my attraction to Latin men, he sent me a few smiley icons.

Sensing an unmistakable connection, I mustered enough courage to ask him if I could call him.

He replied, "I would like that. But let me call you."

Perhaps he was protecting his identity more than I was. I'm not sure. He did tell me later that the day we met in person for the first time, he had a pocketknife in his jacket just in case I was a psycho.

After sending him my phone number, I waited in great anticipation for the phone to ring. I paced back and forth. After a few minutes, the silence was broken as the phone rang. I raced to the phone.

"Don, this is Juan."

In my attempt to sound calm, though I trembled with excitement, I greeted him with a soft hello, and we settled into a conversation that lasted into the wee hours of the morning. Convinced there was strong chemistry between us, we arranged to meet the next day.

That first night after I talked to Juan, I couldn't sleep. His Puerto Rican accent echoed over and over in my mind. I tossed fitfully in my queen-size bed as if it were the night before a final exam. My mind raced with anxious thoughts of this Latin man who had stepped into my life. Mesmerized by the electricity I felt during the nearly three-hour phone conversation, I knew a magical connection had awakened something deep inside me.

I lay restless in the stillness of the bedroom of the large ranch-style home, as the minutes ticked slowly by on the clock. It was after 3:00 a.m. I needed to calm myself down and get some sleep. In just a few hours, I would be face-to-face with the man whose English was spoken with a sexy, foreign accent.

Would he like me? Would I like him? How about the attraction, would it be mutual?

Such questions kept running through my mind. Eventually, I drifted off into a deep sleep.

The brilliance of the new day awakened me sometime mid-morning. As the Sun's rays pierced the large bay windows, I stumbled to the bathroom, still groggy, when suddenly, like a lightning bolt, it hit me: *I had a date with Juan today, here in West Virginia of all places. Now, like a dream come true, it was happening.*

Energized, I rushed into this new day. I made some coffee, ate breakfast, and got dressed. All the while, nervous energy fought for control of my emotions.

We planned to meet at Pilgrim Glass, one of West Virginia's most famous glass factories, a local landmark that would be easy for him to find. It would take me about five minutes to drive there. He said he would be waiting at exactly 1:00 p.m.

I enjoyed the autumn breeze that carried the fragrance of dark blue asters blanketing the hills and surrounding gardens as I drove to the glass factory. The palms of my hands were wet in anticipation of meeting Juan.

When I pulled onto the parking lot, my eyes immediately locked onto the light-brown Toyota Corolla sitting by itself on the lot. I pulled beside it. An olive-skinned man with a long black ponytail emerged. *Damn, he is beautiful!* His long black hair glistened in the sunlight. As we shook hands, I was all thumbs.

Stumbling over my words, I introduced myself. When he introduced himself, I loved the uniqueness of his heavy Latin accent.

The attraction was inescapable. He had the most beautiful lips, big brown eyes, and a heavy black beard. He stood about 5' 9", with a medium build, somewhat shorter than my 6-foot frame. I was swept off my feet by his charm.

I stood face-to-face with this dreamy specimen. We talked in the parking lot for what seemed an hour, more likely thirty minutes. He told me about his profession as a nurse. I mentioned to him that I was in customer service for a large pharmacy. After we talked for a little while longer, the attraction was unmistakable.

I was convinced he sensed the intense chemistry between us, so I asked, "Juan, would you like to come back to the house?"

Without hesitation, he agreed. I told him it wasn't far and to follow me. As we pulled out of the parking lot and headed towards the house, insecurity gripped me. I thought *he's not going to follow you.* But even as other insecure thoughts flitted through my mind, I decided to trust in his honesty. I knew he would join me at the house. And he did.

When we arrived back at the house, I invited Juan into the spacious living room, with its two lazy-boy chairs, an L-shaped sofa, and a plush beige carpet. Trying to ease the awkwardness, I asked him if he would like something to drink and he said he would. I hurried to the refrigerator and brought us both back Cokes.

After we perched on the sofa, we made small talk for the first few minutes, chatting about the happenings that had brought us to this point. I told him about my friends T and J whose house it was, and about our close friendship for many years.

As the moments passed, we moved closer to each other. Melting into his strong arms, I gently touched his scruffy black beard. Our eyes met in a prolonged gaze. Then it happened. He leaned over and kissed me. I was swept off of my feet right then and there, as euphoria surged through my body. In that instant, I understood what Carol King had sung about in her classic, "I Feel the Earth Move."

Our mutual attraction paralyzed me.

OUR FIRST WEEK (OCTOBER 15, 2001)

Cupid shot his arrow straight through my heart on that early October afternoon when I first met Juan. Euphoria surged through me as this charming Latino awakened my sleeping heart. The unyielding effect of his first kiss held me spellbound. His suave, sexy complexion, tender lips, long ponytail, and deep brown eyes took my breath away.

Alone with this beautiful man on this warm afternoon, the ambiance of the large ranch-style home and softness of the large cream sofa further relaxing us, as he and I moved closer to one another. Melting into his strong arms, I knew instantly he was exceptional. As I gently touched his lips and felt his scruffy black beard, our eyes met in an extended gaze, mirroring each other's excitement, the attraction paralyzing, moths to a flame.

For over an hour he and I were lost in a consuming passion of erotica. Suddenly, like a lightning bolt, Juan jumped up, muttered a couple of expletives, and hurriedly shouted he must be at work by 3:30, and it was now already 3:00. In a short embrace, we kissed, telling each other what a wonderful time we had. He rushed out the door, vowing to call me later.

For several moments after his car left the driveway, I felt so alone. The house was dead quiet. What had just happened? Was it a dream? Was this white knight in shining armor a hallucination? I could still feel his embrace, smell his scent, so it had to be real.

Meeting a Latino in Huntington, West Virginia, of all places was rare. Huntington is situated on the banks of the Ohio River, bordering the states of Ohio and Kentucky, quite far from any Latin country. In this small city of nearly fifty thousand, there might be two or three gay bars in the whole city. It's a very tight-knit community, for fear of being ridiculed, gay men and women were still quite discreet.

Just a little over a month before meeting Juan, on September 11, 2001, the United States had come under attack by Osama Bin-Laden's militant Islamists, Al-Qaeda. The nation was shocked. The entire airline industry was affected by the tragic consequences that day.

Further compounding my fears of loss and separation, Juan had a scheduled flight to Orlando, FL, a couple of days after we met. Because of the uncertainty of travel safety, I was scared for him to fly. I made him promise to call me as soon as he landed.

Irrational fears plagued my mind the whole time I knew he was in the air. *What if his plane is hijacked? What if it crashed? What if this man who had come to mean so much to me in such a short time was taken from me?* I was so afraid something terrible was going to happen to him, I was racked with anxiety until I heard from him. When he called and let me know that he was okay, peace flooded me.

Throughout the week he was gone we talked frequently about what he had been doing in Orlando. Was he going to Walt Disney World? Universal Studios? What had he and his friend Carmen been doing? I knew they were very close, having gone to nursing school together, so I was very glad they had a week to visit with one another, even though I was very glad they had a week to visit with one another, even though I missed Juan and couldn't wait for him to come back.

Juan had not only gone to Orlando to visit Carmen, who was a registered nurse like himself, but he had given some thought to possibly relocating there. What if he decided to move to Orlando? The prospect of his possibly moving to Orlando concerned me greatly, as I was falling deeper under the spell of this enchanting Latino.

THE PEEPHOLE

Situated on the maple- and oak-lined Sixth Avenue of Huntington, within a short distance of downtown, sits a three-story brick house on a corner lot. On the first floor of this house is the one-bedroom apartment I lived in when I first met Juan.

At approximately eleven fifteen each night, Juan would come by my apartment after his 3-11 p.m. shift at the hospital. On the outside of my door was a peephole that I use to see the person waiting on the outside. A soft knock on the door would interrupt the silence of the quiet night. Peering through the peephole, I would get a glance at Juan's scruffy face staring back at me from the dimness of the hallway.

Swiftly opening the door, I would stand face-to-face with my hot-blooded Latino. Still, in his hospital garb, he would step into my apartment and in a flash fall into my waiting arms. Our lips would touch in a furor of passion.

SPRING VALLEY

Across a narrow bridge, just off Piedmont Road on the west end of Huntington, begins Spring Valley Drive. It's a curvy, winding road, at one juncture close to the Spring Valley Golf and Country Club. Farther out about a mile, on top of a hill, sits the Veterans Administration Hospital.

Juan was a registered nurse with the VA Hospital, renting an apartment less than a mile from the hospital. Because we hated being apart, we decided I should move in. His two-bedroom apartment was spacious, with a living room, kitchen, and bathroom.

It was the fall of 2001, less than a week before Thanksgiving. We'd dated less than a month. Our fiery romance set our hearts aflame. The passion ignited as two worlds collided.

On this mid-November afternoon, on my way home from work, I hesitantly decided to stop by the church my ex-wife and I had attended. Just pulling into their parking lot caused anxiety. Here I was at a church that for years condemned the very lifestyle I embraced. I had no idea what I was doing here. Perhaps I was looking for approval from a spiritual advisor.

I entered the church and said hello to several laypeople on staff at this large Church of God. As I trekked down the hallway, memories flooded my mind of an earlier life where for over fifteen years I sat in the pews of this church, indoctrinated week after week with anti-gay teachings, all the while, the real me sat invisible, ashamed to reveal my true identity.

Now, years later, still vexed by this school of thought, wrong-headed disciplines still find a way to get under my skin. Like a tremor moving along the San Andreas Fault, mind battles I once fought tirelessly about attraction toward other guys, coupled with my inadequacies in fighting off their temptations, flared up. For since my divorce just a few months prior, I'd been successful in pushing these conflicts deep into the corridors of my consciousness. Now, suddenly like an anaconda, they began to strike.

In a deluge, I was abruptly swallowed in memories of the debacle of my marriage to my ex-wife, amid repercussions of how I allowed the opinions and persuasion of others to convince me that marrying her was God's will. Ultimately, I was treated *as persona non grata* by former fellow parishioners.

My visit to the church was brief. I called Juan to let him know I was headed home. On the spot, he sensed something was wrong. My voice cracked, and I was on the verge of tears. I was a ship tossed on an angry sea. I failed miserably at keeping my fractured emotional state hidden. For even in a very short time, he already knew me very well. He knew of my conflicts with my faith. Reassuring him, I convinced him we'll talk when I get home.

Driving home, I could not wait to get there to pour my heart out to him about how I'd been feeling, to feel his love, reassurance. Although anxious to face this conflict, my heart assured me of the warmth and love I'd find awaiting me when I got home.

Entering the front door of our apartment was like walking into a battle zone. Sitting on the sofa was Juan, forlorn, his beard unshaved, the first time I've seen him unshaven, his countenance fallen, so vulnerable.

He asked, "What are you going to do? Are you going to leave me?" My heart sank, my heart pierced by his words. He knew how important my faith is to me.

"How could I leave you? You're the only true expression of love I've ever known. I love you." Compassion overtook me like a tidal wave. I ran to him, sobbing, holding him tight.

A CHANGE IN THE WIND

Juan and I were in this relationship for the long run. Although he didn't have the spiritual conflicts as I did with his faith, this was his first relationship with a man. As the days turned to weeks, and the weeks months, he and I settled into a stronger love for each other.

Eventually, we moved into a bigger apartment on the west side of Huntington. One morning as I made a delivery for the nuclear pharmacy company I worked for, there were white-out conditions because of the intensity of the snow falling. As I drove east on Interstate 64 out of Huntington toward Charleston, WV, the Ford Ranger pickup I drove began to slide. Unable to control the direction of the slide, I crossed the median, slid across the westbound lane, which in better weather conditions would be heavily traveled by trucks.

After I had crossed the westbound lanes of the interstate, I slid down a slight embankment; the truck turned and the front of the truck faced the highway. Amazingly enough, the cup of hot chocolate I had in the cup holder of the truck hadn't spilled. The snow had acted like a cushion as I slid across the median. Truly, the Lord had me in His mighty hands.

I gained my composure and called a wrecker to pull me out of the ditch, then I phoned my manager, Allan, at the pharmacy to inform him of what had happened. What he said to me on that fateful morning left me stunned, "Are you able to complete the rest of your deliveries?"

Taken aback at his lack of concern for my well-being, I assured him I would.

I had heard most of my life that the best way to overcome the fear of something, especially that of an accident in a car, is to get back behind the wheel as soon as possible. And this is exactly what I did. I had two deliveries to make for the pharmacy, and I was determined to finish my shift. I was more careful and by this time, the roads were somewhat clearer.

As fate would have it, this would not be the only accident I would have that winter. On another occasion, light snow had fallen on a state route I traveled in eastern Kentucky, and unbeknownst to me, there was "black ice," which is transparent and forms on the surface of a highway. As I drove north on the state route, after light snow had begun to fall, I slid off the highway and came to a stop less than 200 feet from a railroad track. This was the last straw.

I began to discuss with Juan the possibility of our moving to Florida. I knew he had a good friend in Orlando, and also it was a tropical climate, more like Puerto Rico. It didn't take much convincing to persuade him to move away from the cold climate of West Virginia. After we made a plan, we determined a move date and gave our notices at our jobs. FLORIDA BOUND, EARLY 2003 On a chilly February morning in 2003, Juan and I packed up our belongings, rented a U-Haul, attached it to his car, and headed south to Florida. I followed close behind him in my car. My tabby cat Belle traveled with him. She had immediately warmed up to him. She was still a kitten at this time, and if I remember correctly, Ishe had fun in that drive to Florida.

Once in Florida, Juan and I stayed with a friend of his, Carmen, an RN with a major hospital in Orlando. Having been a Registered Nurse for several years, it didn't take him long to find a nursing position. As a matter of fact, he's with the same hospital to this day.

I worked at a couple of positions before finding one I liked with Event Imaging, a subsidiary of Kodak. I was hired as a photographer with Walt Disney World, a job I thoroughly enjoyed.

During my first year with Event Imaging, I worked at Epcot. On any given morning, you would find me at the front gate, camera in tow, a Walt Disney uniform on, and a big smile.

The park opened at 8:30 each morning. My favorite part of this position each morning was taking pictures of little girls all dressed up in their Cinderella dresses. You could see the excitement in their eyes, and I'll remember these times for as long as I live.

It was not uncommon for me to take 250 to 300 pictures a day. When I was given the chance to take pictures of children with Mickey or Minnie Mouse, the excitement in their eyes was breathtaking.

The focal point in the pictures taken at EPCOT was the Spaceship Earth geosphere, or as most people refer to it, as "the giant golf ball." Many of my guests requested their pictures to be taken in front of the big ball.

I worked for a year at Epcot before taking a transfer to MGM Studios. The focal point at MGM Studios was Micky's Big Hat. I would always ask the guests if they wanted their picture taken in front of Micky's Hat.

Working at EPCOT and MGM Studios provided two of the best years of my life. The job allowed me to meet people from all over the world. But I must say, guests from Great Britain were my favorite. I loved their accents, and they were the friendliest.

Juan and I had settled into a comfortable life in Florida by this time. He had a good position at one of the local hospitals and our love continued to grow, or so I thought.

One day, as I walked into the bathroom at MGM, I was confronted by what you might call, "male erotica." A guy I had seen before at the park propositioned me. Though I turned him down, it was then and there that temptation began to erode the love and attraction that I felt for Juan. In Sarah McLachlan's musical masterpiece, "Fear," she writes, "they say temptation will destroy our love, the never-ending hunger." After this encounter in the bathroom, it seemed as if the gales of temptation had been loosed against me and Juan. The incident in the bathroom bothered me so much that I told Juan about it. I don't know why I felt the need to confess this to him but I do remember his reaction: he cried. If I had this to do over, I never would have told him.

I thought he and I had a perfect romance. He was my prince. But that day in the bathroom, when temptation entered my heart, as I look back now, I know it was then that the love and attraction I felt for him began to die.

For almost two years, I lived with the pain of knowing my love for him had waned, and it destroyed me from the inside out.

CHAPTER 12

DOWNWARD SPIRAL

The downward spiral my life had taken in the three years before my suicide attempt in early January 2009 had brought me to my knees. The break-up of a relationship with my partner, Juan, accompanied by the many years of intense conflicts that arose due to my faith and being a gay man, had finally taken their toll.

Although unfamiliar with the psychological term at the time, I had been experiencing "psychache." Coined by the late Dr. Edwin S. Schneidman, "psychache" refers to the hurt, anguish, soreness, intense, pain in the psyche, the mind. *(See Suicide as Psychache, A Clinical Approach to Self-Destructive Behavior by Edwin Schneidman.)*

The harsh psychological pain I experienced was both physically and emotionally debilitating. My nerves were on edge. Anxiety and restlessness ruled my world, and enduring each day became almost unbearable.

My best friend quickly became an anti-anxiety medication, lorazepam. I would have to take a dose before going to work mornings and sometimes another one to make it through the remainder of the day.

My eyes became a fountain of tears at the least recall of the bitter-sweet memories Juan and I had shared. One day, a few weeks after breaking off the relationship, I was putting some files away at the firm where I work. Suddenly, I was encased in the memories of our life together. At the time, Juan had been learning the piece, "Beauty and the Beast," on the piano. In my mind, I was replaying that piece over and over, as tears were flooding down my face, each memory tugging on my heartstring. The effects of these memories were crushing. How I longed to love him the way he loved me!

We had moved to Orlando in February 2003, settling there without a hitch. He had found a nursing position immediately, and I soon found a photography position at Disney. Our life together seemed a dream. We had what I thought was the perfect relationship.

It wasn't long, however, before the insecurities I had battled for so many years began to cause problems. First, it was an attraction to another guy I worked with at Disney, then the realization that my love for Juan was fading. This, accompanied by the continual torment in my mind from years of anti-gay teaching in a strict Pentecostal church, was about to send my emotions reeling.

My dilemma had finally come to a head. I could no longer continue to torture myself about this mountainous impasse between faith and sexuality, and a failed relationship. Something had to give.

The final blow that toppled my house of cards was the realization that the love between Juan and me had died. I was now facing my worst fears. It was all very reminiscent of the poignant ballad by Annie Lennox, "Why," a resonating, profound loss of what had once been a beautiful relationship. She sings, "Let's go down to the water's edge, and we can cast away our doubts." The doubts I had felt about our love were eating me alive.

Our romance had begun like a fairytale. He had been my first love, my prince. Upon realizing that my love for him had changed, I just couldn't accept this fact, no matter how hard I tried.

I would pour myself out to God in prayer, asking Him to restore the romance, the attraction...all to no avail. Even though the romance had been over for some time, I had decided to conceal the truth, not confiding in Juan what was going on for me. The thought of hurting him was just too much to bear.

In the over two years living with this tragic knowledge that my love had died, the secret had become a ticking time bomb, about to explode. The tightrope I had been walking was about to snap.

When I finally did confront Juan with the truth, this just added to my misery. Seeing the hurt and feelings of betrayal in his eyes was more than I could bear. How could I have ever hurt him so deeply? Inflicting this severe heartache on him was the last thing I ever wanted to do. Our life together, once a place of peace and tranquility, had acquired an atmosphere of strife and regret.

Finally, on that fateful Saturday evening, realizing I could no longer endure the agonizing pain of a fractured relationship and a terribly conflicted mind with my sexual orientation and faith, I staggered my way through the dense fog of my emotions into our upstairs bathroom, as if I were walking in slow motion. Without a doubt, contemplating suicide has to be one of the darkest experiences a human can know. It's a time of incredible loneliness. You feel abandoned by everyone, even God, as if you're the only one in the entire universe.

That final moment to end my life had come, the end of the road. My tormented soul was going to find peace at last. When a suicidal person makes it to this juncture, it is finalized. It is settled. For him to execute this final act of misery will be easy, as his relief is in sight. He doesn't see the devastating effect it will have on his family and friends, their grieving. His mind is fixed. He just wants the unbearable emotional pain to end.

After contemplating the final actions for several minutes, I decided on taking an overdose of pain pills. Standing at the bathroom sink, I took one last look at my forlorn image in the mirror. I thought to myself, *so this is how it all ends.* I then put the pills in my hand, took a deep breath, and swallowed a handful of them with a gulp of water. I stood silent for a few minutes, not feeling anything—no fear, no other emotions, nothing.

What happened next was a godsend. I lay down in my bed and hoped to fall asleep, thinking it would soon be over. But then, I felt an urgency to get up. I was in a state of panic. I thought to myself, *I've got to tell Juan what I've done. I don't want to die.* I hurried downstairs where he was watching television and frantically, I told him that I had taken an overdose.

At first, he was angry. "How could you do this?" he cried.

After a minute or so, a sudden calm came over him. The experience he'd acquired over the years as a Registered Nurse had taught him to remain calm in panic situations like this.

He hastily led me into the bathroom and frantically tried to get me to gag by sticking a finger down my throat. When this plan failed after several attempts, he told me to get dressed so he could take me to the nearest hospital. In my panic, I did exactly as he said.

Though a nervous wreck, I hurriedly dressed, and we headed out the door.

The crisp, cold air of that January night engulfed me. The chill cut to the bone. Not a star was shining. The blackness of the night sky taunted me. I felt as if nature itself was laughing at the audacity of my act of desperation.

By this time, Juan's display of anger had transformed itself into one of selfless compassion. The love in his heart for me, even after all the hurt I had caused him, was still alive. We had been together for over seven years. Although deeply hurt by the breakup, this man would prove to be of recurring strength for us both in the coming months.

The stillness was deafening as Juan drove us out of the apartment complex. Few words, if any, were spoken as he drove us as fast as he could to Health Central, roughly a two-mile drive.

Upon arriving at Health Central Hospital, we were greeted with huge, orange rectangular welcoming signs illuminating the lush landscape of a variety of flowers and shrubs; large white arrows guided us on a winding road to the back of the hospital where the emergency room was stationed.

Juan quickly pulled into a parking space and rushed me into the emergency room. He summoned a nurse, telling her that I had taken an overdose. She immediately took charge. After checking my vitals and conducting a thorough examination of my body for other injuries, she had me taken to a bed and given a thin, flimsy blue gown to wear, and I began to shiver. The chill and draftiness of the emergency room, accompanied by the elevated state of my nerves, just added to my panic state.

Next, I was given a black, chalky liquid, containing activated charcoal, to drink. It was nasty. The texture of this liquid would remind me of the Rolaids antacid pills my dad used to take. When administered within an hour of drug ingestion or overdose, oral activated charcoal is effective at reducing drug absorption into the body. After what seemed like a hundred trips down the long corridor of the emergency room to use the bathroom, I was exhausted. By this time, I had successfully drunk a large pitcher containing the liquid with activated charcoal. Throughout the overnight hours, the nasty black liquid had made its way through my digestive tract and bladder on its way out of my body, ridding my body of the drugs I had ingested. It seemed every five minutes or so I was making my long journey to the bathroom. Having to make so many trips made me self-conscious. It embarrassed me.

During each of these trips, I could feel the whole ER Team watching me, medical hawks tracking their prey-patient. Perhaps I seemed just another failed attempt at ending one's life. Did they really care? If they did, they didn't show it. The absence of any evident concern for me was obvious in their behavior...apathy and insensitivity. No real concern for their patient. Or was it "tough love"? Don't do this again!

I was beginning to feel bothersome to the staff. Each time I would have to go to the bathroom, an aide would have to accompany me down the long hall, then have to wait outside the bathroom door. If I would take too long, they would ask me if I was ok. Such an invasion of privacy! I felt humiliated.

Finally, the two quarts or so of the black, chalky liquid had made its way through my body. Now it was daylight. The ER was alive with staff changes. A very long and exhaustive night it had been for me. I'd been in the ER for over eight hours and hadn't been able to sleep.

Sometime during the night, hospital personnel had suggested to Juan that he leave the ER and go home. So focused on my issues, I had failed to take into account Juan's needs. How utterly selfish I had been! Now, I wanted to see him desperately, to tell him I was sorry, but they wouldn't let me. *How is he doing? I've just got to know.* Soon, my mind fixated on Juan's well-being.

Later that morning, a mental health representative began interrogating me. Although the questioning was per protocol, it felt ruthless.

"Why did you take an overdose?" she asked. "How many did you take? Have you tried this before?" Endless questioning! Finally, after what seemed like hours, she stopped.

This whole interrogation process had been quite exhausting and challenging. Having to come face-to-face with a near-fatal attempt at overdosing on a handful of pain-killers forced me into an encounter with my mortality. Had I wanted to die? Could I survive this continual mental torment? What about the ones I loved and those who loved me? My precious mother, for instance. How was this going to affect her?

Still, however, my psychache had blinded me to these ramifications. I had come to this crossroads because of severe anguish. Pain so debilitating, I didn't want to go on living. I wanted the pain to end. Continuing to live meant more pain. Could I endure more pain? What quality of life would I have? What steps would I have to take to find a peaceful resolution?

Not long after I had been admitted to Health Central, Juan had notified my boss at the law firm where I was a records clerk, of my suicide attempt. Craig was a very understanding guy, a compassionate man. His main concern was that I receive the care I needed to get better. He assured Juan that my job was secure and for me not to worry.

Not many days later, I was placed on the Family and Medical Leave Act. The Family and Medical Leave Act (FMLA) provides an entitlement of up to 12 weeks of job-protected, unpaid leave during any 12 months to eligible, covered employees for the following reasons:

1) birth and care of the eligible employee's child, or placement for adoption or foster care of a child with the employee;

2) care of an immediate family member (spouse, child, parent) who has a serious health condition; or

3) care of the employee's serious health condition.

It also requires that the employee's group health benefits be maintained during the leave. The Family and Medical Leave Act is administered by the Employment Standards Administration's Wage and Hour Division within the U.S. Department of Labor.

I had been with the law firm for over five years, was well-liked, appreciated by the whole staff. What a comfort it was to know that I didn't have to worry about losing my job. Truly, I was blessed to work at a firm with such caring aspects.

Working towards a peaceful resolution to my emotional problems would prove to be a major challenge in the coming months. Subsequently, these challenges would once again cut me to the core of my being.n.

Sometime after this strenuous interrogation by the mental health professional, arrangements were made to transfer me to a mental health facility in Kissimmee, the standard protocol after a suicide attempt.

The Florida Mental Health Act of 1971, commonly known as the "Baker Act", allows for the involuntary institutionalization and examination of an individual, and can only be initiated by judges, law enforcement officials, physicians, or mental health professionals.

Under the Baker Act, for the person to be institutionalized, there must be evidence that the person:

- Has a mental illness (as defined in the Baker Act)
- Is a harm to self, a harm to others, or is self-neglectful (as defined by the Baker Act)

Juan had made it back to the hospital sometime during the early morning hours and was waiting in the ER waiting room. Shockingly, when I asked to see him, the hospital refused to let me.

Why wouldn't they let me see him? I cried. Perhaps it was because he wasn't family or next of kin. I didn't know, and they wouldn't tell me. I felt even more alone. The only person I could count on, the only person I knew, who truly cared, was suddenly not allowed to see me. It was *déjà vu*, reminding me of the steps leading to my suicide attempt, and a dark cloud of despair once again began to envelop me.

When it came time for the ambulance to transport me to a mental health facility in Kissimmee, I begged and pleaded for them to let Juan go with me, to let me see him before I was taken away. They denied the request. In my weakened mental state, I just couldn't understand why the hospital was being so mean, so calloused. Once again, the hospital was simply following protocols in the Baker Act.

Upon being told I was being transported to Kissimmee, and that he was not allowed to see me before I left, Juan was overcome with emotion. I will never forget the so-sad chance encounter we had as we passed by in the hallway on my way out of the hospital. His sobs were uncontrollable. His forlorn appearance, his look of being abandoned added to my misery. Devastated at seeing him like this, I felt helpless. This pitiful sight, etched in my memory, will haunt me to my dying day.

Once again, despair grabbed my psyche. I was riddled with guilt. This whole nightmare had been my fault. To see Juan be in such agony worsened the situation.

I was confined to an ambulance and began the long trip to Park Place Behavior Health Care in Kissimmee, roughly an hour's drive from Health Central Hospital, just west of Orlando. It was a journey I will never forget, with tormenting images of Juan's desolate facial expressions and heartrending sobs. Suddenly, I became fixated on his welfare. *Where is he? Is he following the ambulance as we drive down the turnpike?* By clinging to the least little thread of hope, I convinced myself that he was somehow following us. He just had to be! Paralyzed with fear and worry, I hoped he had composed himself enough to make the drive. For the next hour, throughout the long journey to Kissimmee, from the back of the ambulance, I kept a determined lookout for his car. The ambulance weaved in and out of traffic, and there was no sign of Juan's black Nissan Altima.

Suddenly, I felt like a caged bird. Humiliation hung over me like a storm cloud. The two paramedics who were seated in the back of the ambulance to guard and watch over me made small talk. I could tell they were trying to cheer me up. However, I could sense they hadn't had much experience in transferring patients in my predicament. *What do they think of me? Do they think I am crazy?* My insecure mental state made it easy to feel this way.

Upon arriving at Park Place, I was led into what I perceived to be the basement of a three-story white building. It was not your typical mental health center, more of a facility for runaways or perhaps drug addicts. Upon being admitted, I was introduced to the Director of Mental Health Services for the facility. She asked me several questions and had me sign a few consent forms, then introduced me to the chaplain, an older, distinguished-looking Black gentleman.

"Do you have a religious preference?" He asked me.

"I was a Christian," I said

He then asked me if I would care if he said a prayer with me. I assured him this was ok. After a brief prayer, I had the opportunity to tell him what was so troubling in my life, explaining that my life was in utter chaos by having this consuming conflict with being gay and being a Christian. I further explained to him about the turbulent road my life had been on the prior few years. Being very understanding and attentive, he instantly came across as a man of great compassion, not judgmental.

After a short time with the chaplain, I was delighted to see Juan standing in front of me. So elated, I hugged him as tight as I could, never wanting to let him go.

We asked to be left alone for a few minutes; the chaplain, a little reluctant, granted us about ten minutes together. Not long after this short visit, he asked if we were related. We explained to him that we were partners. Being okay with this explanation, he then told us that visiting hours were over.

It was time for me to be admitted. Instantly, my tears welled up. "When will I see you again?" I asked Juan. "Are you going to be ok?"

He assured me that he was alright. He promised to visit as often as he could over the next three days. According to the requirements of The Baker Act, a person must be examined for up to 72 hours after he is deemed medically stable.

I was instructed to say my goodbyes to Juan and quickly led into a very bare, cold environment. As I entered this brightly lit, white room, the door closed loudly behind me. Suddenly, I had the gut feeling I was locked up, detained against my will. A prisoner. Now in a place of no emotion, I was greeted with empty stares and hollow greetings.

Unbeknownst to me, I would spend the next three days there, not quite the setting I had visualized. I imagined more of a hospital set-up. This was more like a college dormitory: large rooms with tile floors, locks on each door, a larger room resembling a conference room, and offices for the mental health professionals.

After a few minutes, I was introduced to the mental health professionals who attended patients daily. Although they were nice and cordial, I immediately felt their scrutiny. One of them told me it was wrong to attempt suicide. "You will go straight to Hell for committing suicide," he said.

From that moment on, I tried to keep my distance from this man. I surely didn't come to this facility to be judged.

The first evening there, all I could think about was wanting to be alone, to sleep. I was exhausted. I had been awake for days. However, this wasn't going to happen. The mental health professionals made sure each patient didn't spend a lot of time alone.

I was assigned a roommate. They explained the rules of the program and told me about mealtimes. Then I was shown my room, a large white room that contained two beds, similar to twin beds, and one window. The bathroom was very small, with a tiny shower and toilet. I was struck with how very impersonal it all seemed, how very cold. The smell of the facility reminded me of my first elementary school, new classmates, unfamiliar surroundings, painful memories of having to be dragged to school, only to be abandoned, or so it seemed, by my mommy. How I hated those foggy mornings of my first years of grade-school in West Virginia back in the middle 1960s! Now, suddenly, these early childhood memories came back, haunting me.

For three days I endured the daily grind of meetings, group participation, and counseling. In the evening, I was allowed to make one phone call to the outside, that being either family or a friend. The only two people I remember talking to on the phone were Juan and my brother, Stan. Hearing their voices was so very comforting to me.

Throughout these long days, all I could focus on was getting through the seventy-two hours. I felt I was going stir-crazy; being treated like a psycho was beginning to have its effect on me. Each of us in the facility was closely guarded. Even going to the bathroom was closely monitored. Every single move was kept track of.

In each of the group participations, it wasn't so much the fact that I felt superior to others, but rather that I didn't know why the other patients were there. *What type of mental illness did they suffer from? I wondered.* I had failed to realize the direly emotional state I had drifted into. It still hadn't dawned on me how critical my condition had gotten.

Most of the other patients were very nice. A few, however, appeared to be more disturbed than others; still, the patients who appeared to be schizophrenic when mumbling to themselves, even they didn't hurt anybody.

Soon enough, it came time for me to leave. When being told that I was going to be discharged from the facility, having successfully fulfilled their criteria to be released, I knew Juan would be there to pick me up. I couldn't wait to see him.

Suddenly, I felt tremendous relief, the first bit of excitement I'd felt in a long time. I was going to see a familiar face. I was going to see Juan once again.

The last hour in the facility seemed an eternity, each minute passing like the sands in an hourglass. When the time did come to leave, I signed the release forms, walked out to the front of the facility, and was overjoyed to find Juan waiting for me. As we drove away from that place of abandonment, I had never felt so free!

It wasn't long, however, before the demons I had fought over the previous seventy-two hours began once more to torment me. The peace I had experienced was short-lived. I soon realized that the instability of my emotions had to be dealt with.

Park Place had recommended I seek further psychological counseling, and I knew they were right. I was emotionally unstable. What was to prevent me from having another meltdown, a second suicide attempt? Although I had shown improvement over the three days while a patient at Park Place, I still desperately needed help to confront my underlying mental health issues.

Over the next few weeks, Juan and I decided on a plan best for my mental health. The plan we chose turned out to be one of continued challenges and onslaughts, further testing our fragile relationship and love. Soon we would be forced to live almost a thousand miles from each other, a distance that would bring a continuation of anguish and new heartbreaks for both of us.

RECOVERY IN WEST VIRGINIA
Taillight in the Dark

Because I had been temporarily placed on the Family Medical Leave Act, to recover from my suicide attempt, my position at the law firm in Orlando was secure. Over the next couple of weeks, Juan and I made plans to move me back to West Virginia, where I could be with my three older brothers, my mom and stepfather, and my younger sister. Although this was the most logical move, it was also the most difficult. Having to move nearly a thousand miles from friends, co-workers, even the animals I loved very much, and from Juan, made me feel quite displaced.

Changes were happening so fast, as if I were on a roller coaster, ups and downs, sharp turns, curves in the road, and my head was spinning. Only my daily dose of anti-anxiety meds and anti-depressants helped me to cope.

In the two-bedroom townhome Juan and I had shared over the previous five years, if you could hear the walls talk, what tales would have been told! There had been good times and bad times, moments of anger and betrayal, and moments of great intimacy. But now, the time had come to move on. Circumstances beyond our control had forced our hands.

It was now time for us both to displace the association we had with this townhome that had been our place of refuge. Attempting to move on, we found that the memories from our time there made packing up our belongings a very toilsome effort. Everything had such strong emotional attachments, it was like ripping a page out of the book of one's life, uprooting layers upon layers of emotions. Such damage would take years to heal.

We spent the last night in our townhome finishing packing. I was packing what belongings I could take with me into my Ford Focus, while Juan was packing his things into a U-Haul, to take to his new apartment in east Orlando. By the time we had finished, it well past midnight, and we still wanted to get a good night's sleep. Our goal was to unpack his things into his new apartment the next morning and be on the road by eight or so with the remainder of my things in the U-Haul and Ford Focus. When we did finally get everything packed, we were both exhausted.

After sleeping on a mattress that last night, and then taking boxes to his new place, we began the long, tiresome journey to Huntington, West Virginia., a road trip that would prove to be a far cry from a joy ride or a vacation. Regrettably, it turned out to be one of the most excruciating trips either one of us had taken.

Getting an early start the next day didn't happen. By the time we did get on the road, it was well into the afternoon. With Juan leading the way in the 16-foot U-Haul, I followed close behind in my Ford Focus. The route we had decided upon took us up I-95 north, then over I-26 east towards Columbia, SC, then north up I-77 into West Virginia. Not only was this an exhausting trip because of our tense emotional state, but the weather proved to be a negative factor also.

Dusk shrouded the landscape by the time we made it into South Carolina. By the time we made the transition from I-95 north and turned west on I-26 toward Columbia, night had fallen, and the temperatures as well. There was bareness to the land. I felt so alone in my car. I was fortunate to have one of my tabby cats, Daphne, with me. How I enjoyed her company! She gave me such warmth and love on this long trip home.

It wasn't long however before thoughts of Juan began to fill my mind. His love for me had been so selfless, so pure. All I could think of while trying to focus on driving was the incredible kindness he had shown to me. I grieved deeply over how I had hurt him. I was so sorry I had put him through all this pain and agony. Although my attraction toward him had played out, I still loved him very much. Just how much I still loved him would prove itself more agonizingly than ever before.

The blackness of the landscape as we drove along I-26 was eerie. I followed closely behind Juan along this deserted highway. I noticed that one of the taillights in the U-Haul was burned out. To me, this dark taillight had a deeper meaning, a symbol of our relationship over the years. For, in a sense, I felt all that we were going through together, the intense heartache and suffering were symbolized by this burned-out taillight, indicative of our lives together. Not exactly: although our relationship was faltering, there was still a flicker of mutual love burning. We had spent seven years building a relationship, and it wasn't going to be lost on the turbulent seas of life in a brief second.

Throughout that long night together, stopping for brief periods to rest and get a bite to eat, we made good time. The weather up to this point had not been too bad. As we got into the higher altitudes of Virginia, the temperatures were much colder. Although the weather was clear, there were telltale signs of prior snowfall along the highway. This meant we had to drive a bit more carefully in these steep terrains.

As we were nearing the state line bordering Virginia and West

Virginia, I found myself in the wrong lane and going the wrong way upon coming to the I-77 and I-81 junction. As I-77 and I-81 forked to the north and the south, I had inadvertently forked to the south on I-81, heading towards Bristol, Tennessee. Upon making this error, I had to drive about 2 miles south on I-81 to make a U-turn. To further complicate matters, the only place to make a U-turn was for official cars only. What did I do? In an almost panicked state, with the adrenaline peaking, I feverishly made the quick retraction and headed back to where I-81 and I-77 forked. It wasn't long before I had caught up with Juan. Fortunately, he had noticed that I had made the wrong turn and was over on the berm with his flashers on, waiting for me to catch up. Smart!

When we finally did make it into West Virginia, it was even colder, and more snow lay on the ground. As we both drove cautiously down the West Virginia Turnpike, with its long and winding four-lane highway, we passed through the West Virginia cities of Bluefield and Beckley. By this time, it was well into the early morning hours, between 4 and 5 a.m., the only sound was that of the tires of our vehicles on the interstate.

Heartbreaking Goodbye

We made our way through Charleston, the capital city of West Virginia, and then it happened. All of a sudden, Juan pulled over to the side of the road. Something was wrong. But what was it? Unsure as to what had happened, I slowly pulled up behind him, put on my emergency flashers, and cautiously walked up to his truck. What I encountered shook me.

Juan rolled down the driver's side window of the U-Haul as I walked closer. When I was within a few feet of the truck, I heard intense sobbing coming from inside the cab. There sat Juan, almost in a fetal position, tears rolling down his face, convulsing, exclaiming, "I can't do this!"

I was taken aback, speechless, suddenly overcome with fear. What were we going to do? All I could do was pat him on the shoulder, and somehow reassure him that it would be okay. But would it be okay? How much more could either one of us take? How much more could he take? Hadn't I put him through enough? The pressure we had been under had taken its toll. Now our bodies were beginning to show the effects.

Eventually, he regained his composure. After we both had pulled back onto I-64 west out of Charleston, toward Huntington, the remainder of the drive was without incident. When we did arrive in Huntington at about 6 a.m., the streets were snow-covered and icy. Driving on the icy streets was a bit challenging for these two weary travelers. We had driven all night, both of us mentally and physically drained.

We arrived at my sister's house. Mom, older brother Rodney, my brother Kayo, and my brother Harold and his wife were all there to greet me and show their love and support. Perhaps that is the one silver lining in the dark cloud that enveloped me. For if there is one thing I have learned through all of this, love and support foster healing.

The meltdown in Charleston was not the last emotional toll of the night. I was unaware Juan had arranged to fly back to Florida that morning at around 9 a.m. When I learned this, I was anguished. I'll never forget him standing under the threshold of my sister's TV room, with tears flooding his face, motioning for me to come and embrace him. As I held him, we both shook with loud sobs, our hearts breaking.

"O, God, help us!" I cried. I will never forget that moment. We seemed empowered with supernatural strength. For God in His infinite wisdom had displayed His great love and grace to both of us. He mightily supplied the strength for both of us to gain our composure and spend the last few minutes we had together before Juan had to say goodbye and leave for the airport.

Juan's return flight to Orlando was in less than an hour. When it was time for him to go, I grabbed him as if I wouldn't let him go. He reluctantly headed out the door, not looking back. I called him on his cell once more after he had left, just to hear his voice one more time before his flight. I would later find out that through all these tumultuous events, he had almost missed his flight. Oh, what hell he must have gone through! He told me later that for the whole flight to Orlando all he could do was cry

Lying on my sister's sofa, after Juan's flight had taken off, I felt such emptiness. Although I had my two tabby cats, Belle and Daphne, the one man I'd ever loved was soon to be nearly a thousand miles from me. I felt emotionally dead. Adjusting to living without him, not seeing him every day, was going to be harder than I'd ever imagined.

Juan arrived safely in Orlando. A friend of his had picked him up at the airport and agreed to spend a few days with him. The first few days back in Florida, he later told me, were the most difficult. Only his work kept him sane. Although he had Tyler, the Yorkie we had bought together, life would never be the same. For reasons beyond our control, we had been snatched from each other's arms. Only time would heal our hearts. We had to face one day at a time and hope the future for both of us would be brighter.

Being with my sister during those first few weeks after Juan went back to Florida in late January of 2009 was the one place I needed to be. Indeed, being with my family after my attempt on my life would prove to be the antidote that would eventually help cure my troubled emotions.

Curled Up in a Ball

Although my family visit in early February 2009 was good therapy for me, it didn't bring me happiness. I still felt detached and deeply depressed. All I wanted to do was sleep. Somehow, I thought that by sleeping, I wouldn't have to face my problems. Lying in bed for hours on end, tossing and turning, my mind racing a hundred miles an hour, curled up in a ball, was my existence. Moment by moment, I was sinking deeper into despair.

Because of the separation anxiety experienced by Juan and me due to being apart, I now faced new demons. The loneliness was excruciating. Each new day, the drudgery of life was appalling. Anxiety ruled. I had no appetite. To muster up enough energy to take a shower even became a challenge.

I had made my sister's upstairs bedroom my haven. Juan had even made a makeshift clothesline on which to put my clothes. The bedroom was cluttered, my belongings everywhere. I couldn't help but feel uprooted.

By this time, I had been back in Huntington for over two months.

After one very distressing day and trying my darnedest to conceal my true feelings from her when she came in from work one evening, my sister Diane asked me how I was doing. To most of the world I might have been able to keep my feelings hidden, but not from my sister. She was very intuitive. She could tell when something was bothering her brother. She had made the same conjecture on the day I had married the woman who became my ex-wife. She had known as well as I did that marriage was a mistake. She sensed my unhappiness then as much as she did on this day.

That old familiar look of worry crossed her face. Trying to convince her I was okay proved futile. She saw through my mask. When she asked how I was doing; I broke down and started to cry. She at once came over and hugged me.

"Sis, I am having suicidal thoughts again," I said. "I'm scared!"

Hearing these words, she displayed grave concern. "You need professional help, Don. You can't continue to live this way."

"I know I can't. I just don't know what to do."

"We'll think of something."

I knew she was right. I couldn't continue living this way. I desperately needed to get some professional help. To continue on this downward spiral was dangerous. That evening we had a very long, heart-to-heart talk. Discussing various venues for mental health services in the Huntington area, we decided upon Prestera Center for Mental Health Services, a very reputable mental health facility, respected throughout the state. I had gone to Prestera many years before, when I had needed some counseling.

It was settled. That evening as Diane and I sat in her living room, I made the call that would be the catalyst for a whole new approach to my life.

The Path to Emotional Healing

1. Therapy at Prestera

In the fragile emotional state I was in, I lacked the insight to know just how unstable my mental health had become. By contacting Prestera, I set in motion the crucial first step to my emotional healing. A new day was dawning in my life. After scheduling the appointment for the following week, I began to sense a glimmer of hope in my dark world.

The grey clouds that hung so low above my head were slowly beginning to melt away. The desperate straits I had been stuck in were loosening their grip. Although I had a long road ahead of me to achieve the emotional healing I needed, at last, I was gaining a new perspective on life.

Prestera Center for Mental Health Services is located in the eastern part of Huntington. It is a large facility with stately trees and manicured bushes encircling its grounds. It houses a manifold of services for mental health, including therapy and supportive counseling for adults, addiction recovery, and services for children and adolescents.

I arrived early on the morning of my first appointment. After completing the necessary paperwork, I was assigned a psychiatrist for a full assessment, a standard procedure for new patients. After a few minutes, I was introduced to the doctor who was appointed to my case. He was a very nice man, in his early sixties, very distinguished. His office had your typical psychiatrist feel, adorned with various diplomas hanging on the wall, both medical and psychiatric academic achievements. The shelves of his office were lined with an array of books covering a multitude of mental health/psychiatry-related fields. After introducing himself and having us get acquainted with each other, he then began an assessment of my current mental health.

He then analyzed the assessment and asked a battery of questions, and he appraised the medicines I was taking. One particular drug I had been taking was Olanzapine (Zyprexa), an anti-psychotic. It had been prescribed by a psychiatrist in Orlando a couple of years before. However, this new psychiatrist had reservations about this drug for me and discontinued its use. He assured me that I displayed no signs of being psychotic and therefore didn't need the drug.

Another drug I was taking was Citalopram (Celexa), an anti-depressant. This drug had worked well for me over the last several months, so the prescription was renewed.

This doctor had a very good bedside manner. The conversation we shared was light and witty. His demeanor was upbeat. His questioning was direct, yet with compassion. I didn't feel intimidated by him at all. He was very down-to-earth. We spent the last few minutes discussing the course of action he felt appropriate to my case. Before adjourning our visit, he referred me to a counselor at Prestera he thought would be best suited for me. Her name was Michele. I would meet with her for the first time the following week.

After this initial visit to Prestera, I was greatly encouraged. Spending over an hour talking with a psychiatrist had lifted my spirits. I fully trusted his evaluation of my mental health status and his recommended course of action. I looked to the future with a brighter hope. I would now set my sights on the upcoming counseling session with Michele, an appointment I awaited with confidence and excitement.

That evening I couldn't wait for my sister to arrive home from work so I could share how the appointment had gone. Diane had been very worried about me, so I was excited to give her some good news to ease her mind. Upon telling her that I met with a psychiatrist and that he had performed an assessment and recommended a course of treatments, she breathed a sigh of relief.

"Don, I am so glad for you," she said.

When I told her that I would be seeing a counselor, she was even more excited. We both knew a change wasn't going to happen overnight. All Diane ever wanted for me was for me to be happy. We have shared a deep bond of love between us ever since we both were very young. Although there had been seasons of sibling rivalry over the years, our bond of love was very strong. She assured me that whatever support I needed, she would be there.

Within a week after the first appointment at Prestera, I decided to move in with my mom and stepfather. I made this decision because my twenty-two-year-old niece, Kelli, had decided to move back in with my sister. Diane still had room for me, but I felt it better for her and Kelli to have the house alone. Besides, Mom and Don, my stepfather, had plenty of room. They had a three-story house with three bedrooms on the second floor.

My first counseling session with Michele was ground-breaking. She had a depth of understanding and compassion for the troubling, underlying issues. After laying a firm foundation for our therapy sessions, we discussed how my being gay conflicted with my faith. Because Michele had counseled clients with similar issues, she had great insight into this dilemma.

This was an issue that had divided my church for years. To many of us who'd endured years of conflict and ridicule from mainline denominations, to be rejected by the church was the proverbial nail in the coffin. Although there had been successful attempts by different Christian authors to bring this hotly contested topic of homosexuality to the forefront, it was never without controversy.

The most successful book to challenge the public was Mel White's autobiography, *Stranger at The Gate*. I had read the book many years ago when it was first published. It was cutting-edge theology. In digesting the intimate details Mel shared with the reader, the discourse reminded me so much of myself. He had survived a suicide attempt and had been married to a woman. *Stranger at the Gate* had a depth of understanding and encouragement that so many of us in the church desperately longed for. In his writing, Mel White gave us all a fresh ray of hope. Why should gays be subjected to continued ridicule and rejection in the body of Christ, when Christ's grace was freely given to everyone?

Homosexuality was not listed as the worst of all sins in the canon of scriptures, although many in the church treated it as such. It was time for those of us who just happened to be a little different to rise and be accepted in the body of Christ as children of God, through Christ. (*Galatians 3:26*)

Although Michele had not been familiar with this book and had never read it. I encouraged her to get a copy. Coupled with her having a gay brother, I was confident the book would be a source of great encouragement to her.

We had covered a lot of ground in our first counseling session. After our 45-minute session, we decided that we would meet once a week for the next several months. The cost of the sessions was based on my income, so the expense was very minimal. The sessions turned out to be one of the highlights of those bleak late winter days of the early spring months in 2009. Even living at my Mom's during this time, with love permeating the house, couldn't erase the profound pain I felt.

There were days driving to Prestera when I couldn't wait to get there. Michele had become more than a therapist; she was now a confidant and adviser. I treasured her ability to help me see things more clearly. While she helped me to work through the layers of issues that had led up to the suicide attempt, there would be times when my emotional state was a wreck. I sobbed on more than one occasion. A couple of sessions I even wept uncontrollably. It was during these times when Michele's gifts as an accomplished therapist shined through.

Our therapy sessions included, but were not confined to, discussing events leading up to my suicide attempt. We also talked at length about the demise of my relationship with Juan. Although unaware of it at the time, I had allowed Juan to become the supreme object of my affection. I had allowed him to become the chief focus of my whole life. By so doing, I failed to realize the others in my life who were also important. Most importantly, there was my precious mother, Anna Belle. Mom was close to seventy-six years old by this time and had experienced her share of difficulties.

It wasn't until she met and married my stepfather, Don, that Mom lived the happiest years of her life. In her younger years, while married to my dad, life had been more wearisome. Dad was an alcoholic and did very little to support his family. Because of this, Mom had been the sole breadwinner. She slaved as a cook at a bowling alley in Huntington, working hard for many years to support her five children. Yes, there were days when she was too sick to work. But if she didn't work, we wouldn't have a roof over our heads or food on the table. Perhaps this is what motivated her each day, knowing that her children depended on her. It is for this and so many other reasons that I have had the utmost respect for this woman.

Every son loves his mother, but to me, Mom was my treasure. She was my pearl of great price. She never celebrated a birthday without a knock on the door from a florist delivering a bouquet from me. Loving her came easily. Bringing her boxes of candy, taking her out for shrimp at her favorite seafood restaurant, these were just a few ways I chose to demonstrate my love and appreciation for all that she had done for me. There simply wasn't a woman on this Earth whom I respected more than this woman. And as she approached the end of her life, I was given the good fortune of spending most of 2009 with her at her most cherished refuge, her three-story brick home in the river city of Huntington, WV.

Mom showed incredible support for my being in counseling during this time. She encouraged the sessions. Although I had not discussed with her a lot of the personal issues I faced, she knew I was in dire straits. A mother knows her children. She knows when something is wrong.

I was fortunate to be on very good terms with all of my siblings. Of course, Diane and I were very close. But I also had three older brothers who were deeply concerned about me and wanted to spend some quality time with me.

With my brother Stan, a mere five years older than myself, he and I had developed a very strong bond, a Jonathan/David relationship from *First Samuel* 18:1 in the *Old Testament,* over the years. Stan was not only a brother, he was a mentor. To me, there was not a better example of a man of God than he, a man of integrity and one who had great respect from his fellow man. His prayers for me were very effective. I had survived the breakdown in my life no doubt because of his prayers on my behalf.

My other two brothers—my eldest, Rodney, and my other brother, Harold, just three years younger than myself, loved me greatly and were concerned with my well-being. Allowing them to love me and spend time with them was great therapy for my fractured heart.

Continuing my therapy with Michele's excellent counseling techniques, I was able to alter the focus of my emotional issues to other just-as-important issues besides the demise of mine and Juan's failed romance. By doing so, I gradually improved, both emotionally and mentally. In time, I grew less and less depressed.

Over several months during the late spring and summer of 2009, Michele and I developed quite a rapport with one another. Every week our sessions began at 11:00, with me always arriving early for the appointments, eager to begin our counseling discussion. Michele greeted me with a smile every time. As we walked to her office, she would ask me about the past week, how I was doing, if anything was new. While making our way into her office, she would quietly close the door behind us.

For forty-five minutes to an hour, we would sit across from one another, as I poured out my heart about what was bothering me that particular day. Never once did she fail in being able to soothe the wounds of my aching heart. Her counseling was impeccable and thorough, so much so, that after several months, I was a changed man.

A Refuge at Mom's House

The decision to move into Mom's house made Mom very happy. Only God knows how worried she had been about me. My mother wasn't a very big woman, about 5'7", maybe 130 pounds soaking wet, grey hair, and marble blue eyes. I was the fourth son born to her and my dad, James Reed Jordan Wilson. My sister was four years younger than I was.

Mom was never one to pry into her children's lives, as she had taught us to be our own person. However, we always knew she was there when we needed her. Many times, I would be sitting at my desk at work in Orlando and I would pick up the phone and call her. Each time she would answer, I'd say, "What's up, Anna Belle?"

She would then say, "What are you doing?"

I always knew she would be there when I needed her. Oftentimes, I would call her just to say hello and that I loved her. Although I hadn't told her about my suicide attempt and the succession of events. her grave concern for her son was apparent.

Mom and I had always been close. I had clung to her tightly as a young child during my first years of grade school, so much so that the first few days of every school year was a traumatic event. Each morning when she would walk me to school, the moment I sensed she was going to leave me, I would burst into tears. An overwhelming sense of abandonment would overtake me. I was held back in the first grade because of not being fully prepared to advance to second grade.

Why had I clung so tightly to my mommy's hand? Why was I so immature as a little boy? I don't know. Perhaps because of the lack of love from my dad, but I'm not sure. All I know is that I was terrified to be out of her sight. I never had this bond with Dad. But with Mom, there was a very special bond. A bond that to this day, although she is gone, is still there.

Mom had always been aware of my ongoing dilemma with being gay and its conflict with my faith. Never once had she shown any type of judgment or difference in her love for me. Her love had always been unconditional. Although I had never been blatant with my sexuality, to her, it would never have mattered. She had known for many years that I was gay, for I had told her that when I was twenty-one. Never once did it make any difference to her. In this respect, I was very lucky. I had gay friends whose parents had all but disowned them because of their being gay, or choosing to be, as some in society would put it.

While enduring one of the worst times of my life, Mom was there to comfort me. Being at her house with its warmth and love gave me a sense of great security. Each morning when I would get up, she, my stepfather, and I would sit at her dining room table and have our morning coffee together. Sometimes I would run and get some doughnuts, teasing my stepfather that if I would give him a dollar, would he eat one. This was an ongoing joke between us. My stepfather, Don, and I were close. He had treated me a lot better than my dad had treated me. I loved and respected him so much.

Mom did her best to keep my mood up. At times, she would ask me if I wanted to take a walk around the block. Having a mother's intuition, she must have sensed that getting outside in the fresh air and sunshine would improve my state of mind and lift my spirits.

She had a big house, three stories. I was given one of her bedrooms on the second floor. During this time, I continued to fight bouts of depression and the desire to sleep a lot. One afternoon she tapped ever so lightly on my bedroom door and asked me what I was doing. Although she didn't want to bother me, at the same time, she wanted to make sure I was okay.

Often, I would stay up late with my stepfather watching television. Many nights after he went to bed, I peered out their front door at my car sitting in front of their house. How I longed to pack all of my things, get in it, and drive back to Florida! Although being in West Virginia during this year was right for me, to this day, I still have recurring dreams that I am in West Virginia, wanting to return to Florida. Some of the dreams have been almost traumatic. Being there against my will during that year impacted me much more than I could ever imagine.

One of the highlights of that year was when Juan visited from Florida. Although he visited a few times that year, there was one visit when he brought his sister, Maria, with him. Mom and Maria hit it off immediately. Being a country girl living in the city, Mom loved to cook. Maria raved about her cooking, especially her homemade biscuits and gravy. Mom truly had a knack for this type of cooking. She could whip up a batch of homemade biscuits in no time flat.

Maria and Juan both grew up in Puerto Rico. Maria had ventured very little out of the country. Aside from the daily sightseeing in and around Huntington during that week, during the evenings we would all play Yahtzee gathered around the dining room table. What a riot! Mom would make a pot of coffee, some type of cake, and often dinner. There were such joy and happiness during these times. We were all so happy. Maria's stay at Mom's house those few days gave her a new perspective on a different way of life than she had known. Although Maria's English was broken, she did very well in speaking Mom's language.

The remainder of that year at Mom's I met with some difficulty. One of the worst times was when I was waiting for my unemployment checks to come in the mail. By this time, I was in dire straits financially. I had gone through my savings. As much as I hated to, I had to ask her and my stepfather for money to hold me over. I will never forget that afternoon standing before them both confiding to them that I needed to borrow money. It was one of the hardest things I've ever had to do. I poured my heart out to them as they sat at their dining room table, tears running down my face.

Their response was one of simple compassion. "Don, whatever you need, it's yours."

I sobbed even harder at that moment. This display of love and compassion had a profound effect on me. I was overcome by such love and acceptance. For by their outpouring of love to me, they had taught me a greater love and respect for both of them.

The remainder of that year with Mom was very rewarding in so many ways. She and I would do a lot of running around together. I would take her to do all the grocery shopping, a tremendous load off my stepfather's shoulder. We would take trips up to central West Virginia and visit two of her sisters and one of her brothers. Those precious moments spent with her will be treasured forever.

By the end of 2009, I was ready to go back to Florida. Mom loved me enough to know that this was what was best for me. On the 29th of December, after being in Huntington since late January of that year, I packed up my car, plus one of the cats that Juan had left with me, and I headed to Florida. This was one of the happiest times of my life. Although not knowing what the future held for me in Orlando, one thing I did know: I was going home.

LET IT HAPPEN

It was a cold morning at Space Coast Skydive, 48 degrees Fahrenheit. The weather: clear. Winds: well below the 25-m.p.h. threshold. Butterflies danced in my belly.

Strapped with the proper gear, I walked to a nearby picnic area to contemplate the morning's events. Then it happened. A shot of confidence from my most trusted Confidante, the still, small Voice. "Let it happen," the Voice echoed. My faith in Christ had always been my mainstay in life. From an eleven-year-old boy in a Presbyterian church in awe of the words to the hymn, "Holy, Holy, Holy," I knew at that moment the reality of the presence of God.

I distinctly remember a night in 1985, as I prayed with my friend Mike at the altar, when this still, small Voice called me to the ministry. "I have called you to preach, that is why your faith has been tried," He said.

We've read of the "still small voice" in I Kings, 19:11-13. The prophet Elijah had made enemies in his slaying of the false prophets of Baal. Shortly after, Jezebel sent a message to him: she will kill him. The prophet, on the run, came to a juniper tree and bemoaned his plight. He sat down and unwisely wished he could die. (How many of us have done the same thing, when we have allowed fear to intimidate us?) Not long after this, Elijah, encouraged by the Lord, stood on Mount Horeb, "but the Lord was not in the wind; and after the wind, an earthquake; but the Lord was not in the earthquake; and after the earthquake, a fire; but the Lord was not in the fire: and after the fire, a still, small Voice." Here, this prophet of God heard the "still, small Voice" of God.

Similarly, on that cold, late-January morning in 2018, as I prepared to face one of the greatest fears of my life, like Elijah, I received a 'word' from the Lord. The word might not have been as spectacular as, "What doest thou here, Elijah?" when Elijah hid in a cave, but I recognized the Voice that spoke to me, and this Voice calmed my fears.

Too many of our lives are motivated by fear. We've allowed the insecurities that have plagued us, insecurities of a lifetime perhaps, to rule over our lives. Author Judy Blume, from her novel, *Tiger Eyes*, about a 15-year-old girl in her attempt to cope with the unexpected death of her father, sums our resolution to combat these fears and insecurities in one simple quote, "Each of us must confront our fears, must come face-to-face with them. How we handle our fears will determine where we go with the rest of our lives. To experience adventure or to be limited by the fear of it."

My fears had ruled my life for too long. And on this 28th day of January 2018, by and through courage and faith in my faith in God, I put my fears to rest. C. Joybell C. said it best, "Don't be afraid of your fears. They're not there to scare you. They're there to show you that something is worth it."

All the fears I faced before that first skydive, as C. Joybell C. wrote, proved to show me that, indeed, jumping from 15,000 feet was more than worth it.

I hadn't always been of such a stalwart disposition. Less than ten years before my act of courage above the Kennedy Space Coast in Titusville, FL, I faced my "dark night of the soul." Sunk in a depression so dark and deep, most days, I couldn't think of a single reason to get out of bed. The culmination of a life of pent-up insecurities, that likely stemmed from religious dogma, had stunted my desire to live. As Sylvia Plath wrote in her masterpiece, *The Bell Jar*, "I couldn't see the point of getting up. I had nothing to look forward to."

It took many months to crawl out of that black hole I had dug for myself. But through it all, I don't think I ever lost hope that the God I had served for so many years, would abandon me. Although I did sympathize with psalmist David in his words from *Psalms 13*:1, "How long wilt Thou forget me, O Lord? Forever? How long wilt Thou hide Thy face from me?" The light of my faith may have flickered, but it never did go out.

In this life I have lived, one thing I've learned is that one must have stubborn faith. We, as Christians, aren't promised a bed of roses. It's quite often the opposite. But we are promised grace. Jesus told the apostle Paul, "My grace is sufficient for thee; for My strength is made perfect in thy weakness."

I've tried to write a memoir from the perspective of hoping to help someone else through what I've been through myself. In *2 Corinthians 1*:3-4, the apostle Paul wrote, "Blessed be God, even the Father of our Lord Jesus Christ, the Father of mercies, and the God of all comfort; Who comforteth us in all our tribulation, that we may be able to comfort them which are in any trouble, by the comfort wherewith we ourselves are comforted of God."

LEAP OF FAITH

As the plane gained altitude, my instructor, Jeff, secured our belts and buckles so that we were in tandem. Once the plane reached 15,000 feet, as a green light flashed, we scooted over to the open door, counted to three, and....

What is courage? Eddie Rickenbacker, a World War I hero wrote, "Courage is doing what you're afraid to do. There can be no courage unless you're scared."

Did I allow fear, as I had done so many other times in life, to deter me from one of the greatest adventures of my life that morning in 2018? No.

I will go nowhere in life if I allow fear to intimidate me. For what is fear, but the absence of faith? One of my favorite passages from the *Gospel of Matthew* is from Chapter 14:29-30. After Jesus startles the disciples by appearing to them as he walks on the sea, he tells them, "It is I, be not afraid."

After this revelation, Peter gets out of the boat and begins to walk on the water to Jesus. Verse 30 reads, "But when he saw the wind boisterous, he was afraid...."

When we worry over the "waves" in our lives, we will most assuredly sink. On the morning of my first skydive, I decided to "Feel the fear and do it anyway." (Susan Jeffers)

There are few things in life more rewarding than overcoming fear. As toddlers, we're afraid to take that first step. But one day, our parents let go of our hand, and we step out on our own. Then a little older, as preschoolers, we have our bike with training wheels. But one day, our parents take the training wheels off, and we're superman.

There are few challenges in life scarier than jumping out of a perfectly normal airplane. The night before my jump, I found a YouTube video about one man's first jump. As I watched this video, I felt a surge of confidence and adrenaline, to the point where I couldn't wait to get to the airfield.

Don't get me wrong: I'm human. Of course, I was scared. Nobody is that brave. What made the difference to me was, I had prayed about the jump, and most of all, I trusted the Lord God that everything would be okay. And besides, as an American author, Mandy Hale, wrote, "It's okay to be scared. Being scared means you are about to do something really, really brave."

In a photo I have, I'm about to jump from the plane. Until one makes their "leap of faith" they will never know what they're capable of. It all lies in facing and then entering the unknown. Once you've made that leap, everything is possible.

All of our lives we lie on the brink of the unknown. On the morning of that great jump from 15,000 feet, once my instructor and I made our leap, our actions were going to have consequences. For almost 60 seconds we fell without the parachute's opening. Luckily, for us, we had a parachute that did open, about a minute into our freefall, and in less than five minutes, we were safely on the ground.

TOUCHING THE FACE OF GOD

December 23rd, 2018, it was eleven months since my first skydive, and as the plane swiftly gained altitude, it became harder for me to breathe. Just four years earlier, I had survived open-heart surgery to repair my mitral valve.

At one of my prior cardiology appointments, I had asked my cardiologist about skydiving. His response, "What the hell do you want to skydive for?"

"I just want to do it," I said.

His answer was approximately, "Go ahead."

As we ascended, the air became thinner, harder to breathe. On that cold December morning of my 18,000-feet skydive, the lightheadedness I felt lasted only for a few seconds, for once we reached 18,000 feet, the green light flashed, and we jumped.

The higher you skydive from, the longer the freefall. From 18,000 feet, my freefall lasted about 80 seconds. Falling at well over 100 miles per hour, I had an adrenaline rush so intense, I momentarily forgot about the parachute. The wind was deafening. Then the parachute opened;

I could have heard a pin drop.

I'll never forget that I breathed through my mouth for most of the freefall. Not a good idea, because once the parachute opened, my mouth felt as dry as cotton batting. I'll not do that again.

I'm not afraid of heights and, unlike my 15,000-feet skydive, my 18,000-feet jump didn't make me nauseous. On my first jump, when the parachute opened, it had twisted and turned somewhat, and the spin made me feel sick. So much so, that if anything had been in my stomach, it would have come up. The second jump, I hardly felt dizzy at all.

I chose to skydive at Space Coast Skydive in Titusville, FL, because of my love for the ocean. The panoramic view of the space coast at Cape Canaveral was breathtaking. A bird's eye view! An "aha" moment, when I experienced a freedom I had never felt.

It's taken me many years to stand up to the giants in my life. Sure, there will still be "Goliaths" to wrestle with, but I can always look back on my life and see how far my courage has brought me. Once we put our faith and courage into action, the sky is the limit.

Actually, even the sky is no limit!

GROWTH THROUGH GOD'S GRACE

In the ten years since my downward spiral period brought me to my knees, there has been substantial growth. Depression is a dark place. I never want to return there. It takes years to crawl out of a hole that deep. But through my stubborn faith and God's amazing grace, I possess a new-found joy in life.

A life-changing experience like a suicide attempt compels one to take an inventory of one's life. For me, the stock I needed, to begin with, was my faith. I had allowed the doctrines of man's interpretation of scripture to infiltrate my belief system. This is scary. The *Bible* even instructs us to guard against such things. In the *New Testament* book of *Ephesians*, it reads, "that we henceforth be no more children, tossed to and fro, and carried away with every wind of doctrine." *Every wind of doctrine*, the apostle Paul wrote to the church at Ephesus. In other words, he is saying for us Christians to be grounded in scripture; to know who we are in Christ.

In the last ten years, I have come to know a God of great grace and mercy. I've also realized that our experiences can help us help others. In the book of *2 Corinthians*, *1*:3-4, it is written, "Blessed be God, even the Father of our Lord Jesus Christ, the Father of mercies, and the God of all comfort; Who comforteth us in all our tribulation, that we may be able to comfort them which are in any trouble, by the comfort wherewith we are comforted of God."

In the depths of my despair, with my suicidal tendencies and depression, if the whole purpose of that has been to write words that help even just one person from taking his or her life, then it's been worth it all. I can best comfort someone when I've been where they are, when I can identify with what they are living through.

For this reason, I've connected with the Central Florida Chapter of the American Foundation for Suicide Prevention. Each November, the Saturday before Thanksgiving, we have the International Survivors of Suicide Loss Day here in Orlando. I've been privileged to facilitate one of the groups in the last few years. I help by giving a different perspective, one from an attempted-suicide-survivor's point of view. At the conference this year, I was privileged to meet and co-facilitate a group with a woman whose husband had taken his life years before, a man who also was gay. He had fought a lot of the same demons I had fought, so I was thankful to reciprocate the compassion and love I had experienced from God back to this precious soul.

The love of God and the gospel of Jesus Christ is all-inclusive. When we get to Heaven, we're not going to find a section for Catholics, a section for Baptists, a section for Presbyterians, etc. No, we're going to find the redeemed, whosoever placed their trust in Christ.

In *John* 3:16, which some call God's most precious verse, Jesus said, "For God so loved the world, that He gave His only begotten Son, that whosoever believeth in Him should not perish, but have everlasting life."

There is a division in today's body of Christ, His church, where some sinners are classified and categorized by degrees of depravity. But I have news for anyone who preaches a doctrine like that. According to *Romans* 3:10, "As it is written, there is none righteous, no, not one....". The gospel of Jesus Christ is for all sinners. "For God sent not his Son into the world to condemn the world," Jesus is recorded as saying, in *John* 3:17, "but that the world might be saved."

The mighty work of grace in my life from that dark night of the soul in January 2009 to where I am today, is extraordinary. I can say without any hesitation that the amazing grace of God has brought me to where I am today now understanding the words of poet John Donne in his magnificent poem, "A Hymn to Christ,"

Though Thou with clouds of anger do disguise

Thy face, yet through that mask, I know those eyes,

Which, though they turn away sometimes,

They never will despise.

PART VI
GOD AND MAN AND LOVE

CHAPTER 13

WHO AM I? WHY AM I? MY STRUGGLE FOR ACCEPTANCE

WHO AM I?

In the mid- to late-1980s, when I rented an attic apartment from a widow on Adams Avenue in Huntington, WV, many a night I listened to the Hosanna Worship CD, *Give Thanks*. As I drifted off to sleep, the soothing praise music filled me with contentment and faith.

In May of 1987, after I had returned from a late-night flight to Huntington from Haiti, I lay on my bed in the stillness of this same attic apartment. Somewhat perplexed, I saw in my mind the faces of the three young children I had befriended on the missionary trip to that impoverished country. There I lay in my warm bed, safely sheltered from the rain and wind, a roof over my head, while these young children in Haiti had to endure the harsh reality of having no running sewer and often lacking the bare necessities of life.

Though we—my immediate family, and I—always had plenty, we were far from rich. We were content. Both my parents had been raised on a farm. Both sets of grandparents had to till the land, raised their live-stock, and they lacked indoor plumbing. Yes, a meager living. I think this is what bothered me so much the night I arrived back in the States from Haiti: I was the lucky one. Or, perhaps these Haitian children were the lucky ones. These Haitians didn't know to have it any bet-ter; whereas, I was rich, according to their standards, but I was not content.

I heard a preacher once expound on the "three Ps" that destroy the faith of the saints: Pride, Prosperity, and Prayerlessness. As I lay there that rainy night in 1987, memories flooded me about the lives of the three children I had met in Haiti. They had never known a differ-ent way of living; yet, they were closer to contentment than most Americans. In America, we are a blessed people. We have better clothes, better automobiles than our parents, and yet we complain. The things we waste should prick our hearts.

In the gospel of *Luke, Chapter 12*, verse 15, Jesus commands:

"Take heed and beware of covetousness: for a man's life consisteth not in the abundance of the things which he possesseth."

As Jesus criticizes covetousness here, in the book of *Philippians, Chapter 4*, verses 11 and 12, the apostle Paul paints a vivid picture of the need for contentment:

"Not that I speak in respect of want for I have learned, in whatso-ever state I am, therewith to be content. I know both how to be abased, and I know how to abound: everywhere and in all things, I am instructed both to be full and to be hungry, both to abound and to suffer need."

Closer to the present, in October of 2016, I experienced a dire issue with my bladder. Due to a botched prostate biopsy, I developed an 80% urinary passage block. I wasn't aware of this until I started seeing blood in my urine. Over the next three weeks, I endured a total of nine catheterizations.

One morning as I lay on my bed, with the pain of a catheter cramping me, the sweetness of the Holy Spirit spoke to me these words about contentment from Paul in *Philippians, Chapter 4*:

"For I have learned in whatsoever state I am, therewith to be content."

Most likely when the Great Apostle wrote these words to the Philippian believers, he was in a Roman prison, with his legs chained, rats running about his feet.

As the Holy Spirit ministered to me that morning in 2016, I realized I could be content in "whatsoever state I am, both how to be abased, and how to abound."

The children I met in Haiti are not rich, but there's a good chance they're a lot more content than are we Americans. Yes, they're impoverished. But one thing they have that most Americans don't: they have contentment. Most likely, they appreciate what they have. Americans lack gratefulness for what we do have. When we learn to appreciate what we have as being enough, we will be a contented, happier people.

Who am I? I strive to be a man of gratitude, living a life of contentment and peace amid conflict. Always at the forefront of my life: what I have is not the best, not the most expensive.

What I have is enough.

I'm content.

WHY AM I?

I stood alone at the top of a steep hill not far from my grandparents' house, in rural, central West Virginia. Under a winter sky, I gazed into a canopy of white, and I shouted "Why?" to God about the familiar, ambiguous desires that had erupted in my twelve-year-old body.

Mentally entangled, I had begun to encounter same-sex attractions. At the onset of puberty, when boys began to notice girls, I had begun to notice other boys. Though many a boy's sexual orientation isn't fully realized at twelve, I knew my attraction was to males.

I had come face-to-face with my Creator a few years earlier. In a Presbyterian church, the words to the hymn, "Holy, Holy, Holy," had unveiled my heart to God and His love. This Christian hymn, written by the Anglican bishop Reginald Heber, emphasizes the Holy Trinity. In the third stanza of the hymn, Heber wrote,

Holy, Holy, Holy!

Though the darkness hides Thee,

Though the eye of sinful man, thy glory may not see:

Only Thou art holy, there is none beside Thee,

Perfect in power, in love, and purity.

In the pew that Sunday morning so many years ago, I gazed over the sanctuary at the stained-glass windows, and I pondered the verse, "Though the eyes of sinful man, thy glory may not see," and I asked myself *what does this mean?* Right then I began my long pilgrimage seeking a deeper meaning of life through Christ.

A sermon I have yet to prepare but one day hope to have the chance to preach will be titled, "How Can Sinful Man Approach a Holy God?" This dark and sinful world desperately needs the redemptive work of Christ to atone for our sins. Those of us who know Christ and have accepted Him as our Savior and Redeemer need to share this "Good News" with those in our lives still in darkness. As Jesus is quoted in *John*, Chapter 3, verse 17, "For God sent not his Son into the world to condemn the world, but that the world through Him, might be saved."

And this verse explains the promise in the verse that precedes it, "For God so loved the world that He sent his only begotten Son, that whosoever believeth in Him shall have everlasting life."

Who am I? Why am I? I am one of those whom Christ was sent to save and whose belief will ensure I will have everlasting life in the hereafter.

STRUGGLE FOR ACCEPTANCE

One by one, my young classmates, some I knew well and some not so well, were chosen for the much-anticipated, Friday-afternoon game of dodgeball in gym class. The two captains had chosen their teams, cheered on by yells from team members already picked. There I stood, alone, eventually to be drafted by default to a team that didn't want me.

Not an isolated incident, a struggle for acceptance had become a way of life for me in my days in elementary school and junior high school. A loner most of the time, I had few friends on whom I could count to include me in their circles.

Gym class was not my favorite class! I dreaded it. I knew too well what to expect from cruel classmates who perhaps already saw something different in this skinny, shy kid of small stature. Even at twelve years old, I barely stood 4'11".

Although there were friends of mine in the class, their friendship didn't help much when it came time to choose teams. Cruel classmates, mostly other boys, often degraded me by one word, "sissy." Each time someone called me this, I sank further and further into myself.

To be bullied is terrible. I remember too well my attempts to avoid certain people out of fear. I am angered when someone says that kids who are frequently bullied just need to toughen up and stand up to the bully. It's not that simple.

Perhaps my struggle for acceptance in those early teen years prepared me for my later experiences. But at the time, I needed a sport I could excel in, but not a real contact sport.

My mom was the head cook for a local bowling alley in Huntington. Since an employee's children could bowl for a bargain $0.25 a game, I took advantage of this discount and began to spend time earning bowling money by doing odd jobs at the bowling alley so I could improve my bowling. Throughout the 1970s and into the early 1980s, I excelled at bowling, rolling several 200 games and participating in many state and city tournaments in West Virginia. In fact, in 1969, I won my first trophy at only nine years of age.

West Junior High School had a bowling team one year, and I was excited to be a part of it. This would be one way I could fit in with the crowd and show I was no sissy, that I could be as good as anybody. Through this interaction, I became friends with guys I would never have known.

Everyone wants to feel accepted. I'm so thankful that at a difficult period of my life, I found an activity where I could feel part of the crowd.

CHAPTER 14

EX-GAY: FACT OR FICTION?

For eight years, from 1983 when I was twenty-two until early 1991 when I was thirty-one, I sat single-minded on a pew, every Sunday, determined to get the upper hand on a "loathsome sexual perversion." I was gay, trying hard not to be. Every week, I did my best to adhere to the teachings of the Pentecostal church, convinced that the sin of homosexuality was atrocious and damning.

After receiving Christ as my Savior when I was 23, I zealously devoted myself to the study of the *Bible*. I spent vast amounts of time in prayer and fasted every week. Fasting: to abstain from food for one to three or more meals to seek and draw nearer to God and to gain more control over the physical body. It was considered one of the most powerful disciplines in the Christian life.

I exercised the discipline of fasting quite often back in those days, for usually one or two meals a day. When I was fasting, I often spent a good portion of the time in prayer. When in prayer during these times, I often prayed for loved ones who had not yet accepted Christ as their Savior. Prayer and fasting go hand in hand.

None of these techniques extinguished my desire to be with men.

My thoughts would always return to longing for what I couldn't have, alerting me to the terrors of eternal damnation if I fulfilled these lusts.

The mind-battles that plagued me during these eight years nearly destroyed my sanity as I white-knuckled my way through the temptations of each day. Sometimes when I faced a strong temptation, or simply noticed an attractive man, my heart would sink, and immediately I'd feel discouraged because I still felt attracted to men. When I'd cave in to the desires of the flesh, I would quickly repent, always afraid I'd go one sin too far and be cast into Hell.

During those eight years, I enlisted the help of various ex-gay ministries to deliver me from this supposed immoral sin. The ex-gay movement was in its infancy at this time, with ministries sprouting up all over the country promising freedom and deliverance from "homosexual bondage," as they called it, through Christ. I was especially helped through a ministry in San Rafael, CA, called "Love in Action." I received a great deal of literature and feedback from this ministry.

The teachings of the ex-gay movement seemed to indicate an individual could simply reverse his sexual orientation, or at best, no longer act on his desires. I tortured myself to the point of despair during those eight long years. Since then, I have come to believe that conversion therapy is misleading and untruthful, often leading many of its followers to attempt, or succeed in, taking their lives.

I feel that it's unfortunate and even dangerous that ex-gay, conversion therapy organizations have failed to publicize the dreadful consequences of "conversions" gone awry. Many men and women have succumbed to suicides over the years by attempting to change their sexual orientation. From my own experience, the journey I trudged down this path nearly destroyed my life.

In her article, "Conversion Therapy Survey Reveals Real Harm in Gay 'Cure,'" Lisa Shapiro in the *Huffington Post* says, "In a new survey of people who have undergone a controversial treatment seeking to change their sexual orientation, a gay man described his eight-year marriage to a woman as a 'scam.' Another survey respondent reported self-hatred, isolation, and depression."

The effects of several years of inner conflict over doing my best to change my sexual orientation had scarred my sense of my identity and my mental health.

After many years attempting to change my sexual orientation, I went so far as allowing myself to be urged—it was more like being co-erced—into marrying a woman in May of 2001, a marriage I was reluctant to consummate. After the dissolution of our marriage of just a few months, I met the man of my dreams, Juan, in October of 2001. I believed that I had finally accepted being gay, so I was able to settle into a comfortable relationship with Juan. Eventually, however, the intense conflicts and mind-battles between my spiritual-religious self and the part of me that was happy being gay began to torment me.

This mental anguish happened in different ways. First, the attractions to other men began to cause doubts to arise in my heart about my love for Juan. Then, I had to endure the familiar battles with my Pentecostal beliefs that began to crawl into my mind. The conflict of these two perplexing controversies in my mind set the stage for a dangerous downward spiral that would bring me to the precipice of risking my very life.

In January of 2009, after several years of intense emotional pain, I decided I could no longer endure not only the conflicts with my faith and being gay but also the agony of having lost my love for Juan. The pain was simply unbearable.

On that fateful January evening, I stumbled to the bathroom in our upstairs apartment, took one long, last, forlorn glance at my unhappy face, crammed a handful of pain pills in my mouth and swallowed them. Peering into my motionless face, I felt relieved. Soon I would be free of all the pain I had endured for so long.

The actions afterward seemed in slow motion. I remember lying down on my bed in hopes of falling into a deep sleep. I felt empty, as if I were the only person in the entire universe, but all of a sudden, I felt an urgency not to die. What had I done? I bolted up from the bed, surged down the steps and frantically told Juan what I had done. At first, he was angry, but he quickly adopted a more compassionate tone. After his attempt to get me to expel the overdose failed, he rushed me to the nearest emergency room.

Although the despair and emptiness subsided somewhat during that long night and into the next afternoon at the hospital, my nightmarish journey was far from over. The next evening, I was transported to a behavioral health care facility in Kissimmee, FL. Because of the Baker Act in Florida, which allowed the involuntary institutionalization and examination of an individual, I was confined to Park Place for 72 hours.

The three-day confinement was spent with other men and women who were struggling with their mental health issues. Counseled by therapists and a psychiatrist, at the end of the three days, I was re-leased into Juan's care. At this time, he and I were at a crossroads about where I should go to heal my fractured mental state. Over the next few days, we decided that I should return to my family in West Virginia. Within a week, Juan and I packed my belongings— everything I had—into my Ford Focus and a rented U-Haul, and we took off for West Virginia. As long as I live, I will never forget that journey. An incident that haunts me to this day occurred when I was following the U-Haul Juan was driving. As we were driving through Charleston, WV, suddenly he pulled the U-Haul over to the side of the road. As I cautiously exited my vehicle and approached his driver's side, I could hear him sobbing.

I asked him what the matter was. "I don't think I can do this," he said, continuing to sob. I quickly realized that after being so consumed with my heartaches throughout the ordeal, I had failed to see his path of pain. I had failed to see how his heart was breaking. After consoling him and convincing him that everything would be okay, I continued with him to my sister's house in Huntington, about an hour away. We arrived at Diane's house shortly after sunrise.

The worst part of the trip was when Juan had to leave me in Huntington later that morning to fly back to Orlando. I will never forget the forlorn look on his face as he tearfully walked out the door with my older brother to go to the airport. At that moment, I understood what Toni Braxton meant by the title of her heart-rending ballad, "Un-break My Heart."

Although I was back in West Virginia with my family, my suicidal tendencies had not ended. The pit of depression I had sunk into was a chasm too deep to crawl out of except one step at a time.

On a bleak, brutally cold, winter evening after moving to my Mom's house, I tried to escape the effects of unbearable pain in the mind, by stealing away into my Mom's computer room. All of a sudden, I caught myself gaping over the edge of the desk into a deep, profound abyss. A place of depleted joy, I don't think I had ever felt so godforsaken.

The stillness was deafening. I felt miles away as if lost in deep space, far from mankind. The emptiness of life enveloped me. I sat gaping into this abyss for what seemed like hours but was only a few minutes.

Suddenly, I was propelled into awareness of the life around me: the bright lights of the computer room, the heat of the furnace, and the endearing, enduring presence of my mother's love that permeated the house. My hope for living renewed, in one split second, I escaped the jaws of despair into the land of the living. Feeling alive for the first time in months, I wanted to shout from the rooftop from the exuberance of joy that had flooded my soul.

I felt enveloped in the light of God's love, as if the radiance of His love had once again risen over my life, like the rising of the morning sun. I knew His presence had delivered me from the pit of despair.

Being there in Mom's house was the best therapy I could have ever asked for. Looking back, now that she is gone, I find it even more important that I was able to lean on her, and that she could support me as I healed.

Today, I try to pay back my gratitude by being involved with the American Foundation for Suicide Prevention. Every February, I participate with the Central Florida Chapter of the AFSP in the "Walk Out of Darkness" here in Orlando. Joy restored to my life, I now have a new purpose and a goal: to help others.

I am currently writing my memoir about my tortured journey to find peace and acceptance with my faith and being gay.

Along this journey of life, the road is often traveled on rocky, steep terrain. As Tom Hiddleston said, "You never know what's around the corner. It could be everything. Or it could be nothing. You keep putting one foot in front of the other, and then one day you look back and you've climbed a mountain."

At fifty-nine, a couple of years ago, I finally solved the "ex-gay: fact or fiction" riddle in my life: I am happy being the gay man I was intended to be.

CHAPTER 15

LETTER TO MY AUNT

Adults must be much more careful than they usually are when criticizing children, especially when implying the child has a fundamental shortcoming. Four decades after she had insulted me as being a "sissy," I wrote a letter to a relative whom I shall call "Suzanne." I was proud of having sky-dived, and I wanted her to know I saw it as a refutation of her careless slur.

Suzanne,

You are probably going to be as surprised to get this letter as I am to write it. I've wrestled with the idea of writing it and sending it and have decided it is best to do so. Sometimes we need to get things off our chest, so to speak.

Over the last four-plus years, I have uncovered lots of memories, some not so good, as I write the memoir about my coming to terms with my faith in God and Christ and being a gay man. It's not been the easiest process but one of great healing.

Our lives are shaped by the experiences we've had. Yours and mine. You no doubt had a mother and father who loved you immensely.

Brothers and sisters who loved you, forming you into the woman you are today. Mom had told me stories of all of you growing up, memories she cherished. I know you must have a lot of memories of her as you look back over the years. I know you miss her. I do each and every day of my life.

My life also was shaped and still is by the experiences I've had over the years. You know as well as I do that I had a mother who loved me greatly. I had the best Mom I possibly could have had. All five of us did. My relationship with dad, not so much. I would like to think had he lived longer, our relationship would have flourished. My relationship with my three older brothers and Diane is excellent. Since losing Mom, we have developed a strong bond. Not that we weren't close already, but through the love we had for her, we have grown closer.

There's an old nursery rhyme, "sticks and stones may break my bones, but names will never hurt me," and I'm sure you've heard it. What I'm about to tell you is not to hurt you, it's something I need to get off my chest. It is something that you said to me some forty-six years ago. It's likely you don't even remember saying it. But you know, the mind, memory, is a powerful thing.

Your family lived on West Avenue, I believe it is, in E****. I was visiting one summer. I was 12 or 13. [One of the children] had a hamster, gerbil, not sure what it was. I was asked to pick it up. Being the shy kid, I was, and quite timid, I was afraid to pick it up. It was then that you said the following words to me:

"Don, you're nothing but a damn sissy."

Suzanne, I have never forgotten those words. Yes, I've forgiven you for saying them. And as I said, most likely, you don't remember speaking them to me. But I do. Words cut. Words hurt. Words have a way of helping to mold us into the fabric of what we are. I am not saying you had anything to do with the man that I have become, not at all.

But these words were powerful when spoken to me.

You might remember, about a year and a half ago I called you one Sunday as I was driving over to visit D*** M***'s aunt. I wanted to tell you what your nephew D** had done. You asked me what did I do? I then told you that I had skydived from 15,000 feet. I must be honest, the only reason I called to tell you that was because I wanted you to know that I was no damn sissy.

Suzanne, I hold no ill will towards you. I send this letter to you in love. You have always held a very special place in my heart. The writer of the book of *I John* said, "If we can't love our brother whom we can see, how can we love God whom we haven't seen." I do love you.

James 5:16 says, "Confess your faults one to another, and pray for one another, that ye may be healed."

Suzanne, please know that I am not sending this letter in any way to hurt you. It is only a way to move on. I probably should have unburdened this issue many years ago.

I pray for you and your family.

Don

CHAPTER 16

LESSONS LEARNED

"Nothing prepares you for this," I repeated to myself over and over that first week of October 2012. My precious Mom lay in her hospital bed, weakened each day by stage-4 lung cancer and an acute case of pneumonia.

On Tuesday morning that fateful week, my sister Diane and I had the grim task of telling Mom that her cancer was terminal. At first, she didn't want to accept the diagnosis, instead, asking for surgery. When we told her surgery was out of the question, she never mentioned it again. For as long as I live, breaking this dire news to the woman who meant most to me will not be forgotten.

Each day that week, my siblings and I did our best to keep Mom's spirits up. Her four sisters came to visit, as did one of her brothers. She was showered with flowers and love. My oldest brother, preacher Kayo, prayed often with Mom to strengthen and comfort her, which she gladly accepted.

Early Friday afternoon, I had gone to my sisters to take a nap. Sometime around 2:30, my older brother Harold woke me to tell me that the doctors had given Mom less than twenty-four hours to live, words to be etched indelibly in my memory.

When we arrived at the hospital, we were told that Mom's numbers had been dropping all day because of pneumonia. After we all had a chance to say goodbye to dear Mother when her death was near, we, her five children and her grandchildren, encircled her bed on that Friday evening, October 5, 2012, to pray for this beloved matriarch. My brother Kayo led us in prayer. When we had said "Amen," Mom was gone. From that day until this, over seven years now, God's peace has carried us.

Jesus said in *John 14:27*, "Peace I leave with you, my peace, I give to you; not as the world gives, do I give to you. Let not your heart be troubled, neither let it be afraid."

Though there is nothing in life to prepare you for the death of your mother, we do have the promise that God's grace is sufficient. For as Jesus told the apostle Paul in *2 Corinthians 12:9-10*, "And He said unto me (Paul), 'My grace is sufficient for thee; for My strength is made perfect in thy weakness.'"

There have been many lessons learned in my fifty-nine-plus years on this Earth, but one lesson, in particular, is about contentment. In 2016, I had a prostate biopsy. Unbeknownst to my urologist, I had been taking a baby aspirin once a day. Because of this, my blood was thinner than normal, and I was more likely to bleed. While in surgery, somehow my bladder had been nicked. A day or so after the biopsy, I started passing blood in my urine. Alarmed, I immediately drove to my urologist's office. After having a bladder scan, and having been told my bladder was empty, I was puzzled, because I knew my own body, and I knew something was wrong.

I left this doctor's office and came home. After I arrived home, my manager called me on my cell. After a short conversation with her sharing the events of the afternoon, she called her urologist who was treating her for kidney stones, and he suggested she bring me in as soon as possible. The revised diagnosis: I had developed an 80% blockage in my bladder. I needed to have an immediate cystoscopy performed. My manager, Terri, may have just saved my life that afternoon.

After a five-day hospital stay and having endured nine catheterizations, I finally began to heal. One morning, as I lay on my bed catheterized, in much discomfort because of cramping, the sweetness of the Holy Spirit spoke to me a verse from *Philippians 4:11*, "For I have learned that in whatsoever state I am; therewith to be content." Suddenly, peace filled my soul. Most likely, when the apostle Paul penned these words to the church at Philippi, he didn't write them from a five-star hotel, more likely from a prison cell. Learning to be content can be attained in this world, but it takes a definite trust and assurance in God that everything is in His firm control.

I've told many friends and family members I would like to come to the place where things I can't control don't bother me. I'm not there yet. Someone has said, "Whatever is bothering you right now, forget about it, take a deep breath, and trust God." This is the best advice I can give.

In October of 2014, I had to do just this. After several heart echocardiograms, I was alerted by my cardiologist that I needed open-heart surgery to repair a severe leakage of my mitral valve. I scheduled a follow-up appointment with a cardiothoracic surgeon; we sat face-to-face in his office in Orlando, FL, and he looked at me sternly and said, "Don, this is serious surgery."

I replied with something like, "I know it is, but if it has to be done, let's do it." We scheduled the surgery a month in advance, and then he and I began to talk about life, and especially about each other's faith. I was able to share with this surgeon my faith and trust in Christ and my firm belief that God was in control.

Before I left his office that morning, this surgeon looked at me and said, "Don, if you don't mind, I would like to pray with you." I agreed. This shot of confidence from a doctor who was going to stop my heart, while performing a dangerous procedure on one of my heart valves, gave me the courage I needed to withstand the doubts and fears that would plague me over the next thirty days. It has now been over five years since my chest was pried open. My mitral valve is performing with no problem.

I've often told people, "If you don't think life can turn on a dime, you haven't lived long enough." We might not be able to stop adversity from coming into our lives, but we can control how the adversity affects us. Through trials and tribulations, we develop character. If our faith is never tested, how would we know we had any? Better yet, how would our faith become stronger?

Like anyone else, I have made my share of mistakes in this life. And hopefully, through them, I have learned some valuable lessons. But I often tell people that if I could go back and change things, I don't think I would change anything. Why? Because God's grace has made me who I am today.

Thank you, Lord.

AFTERWORD: GAPING INTO THE ABYSS

The connotation of the word "gaping" implies to stare with open mouth, as in wonder, to open the mouth wide involuntarily, in absorbed attention. In January of 2009, my experience with gaping was one of great bewilderment and abandonment.

Those days were tumultuous. I had survived a suicide attempt nearly a month before. My life was in such disarray, the storms raging inside had shaken the very foundation of my being.

On a bleak, brutally cold, winter evening, I tried to escape the effects of psychache, the unbearable pain in my mind, by stealing away into my Mom's computer room. I found myself transcending into a most empty sense of existence. I caught myself gaping over the edge of the computer desk into a profound abyss, a place of such depletion of joy, I never felt so godforsaken.

The stillness was deafening. My senses seemed miles away, as if I were lost in deep space, far from any existence of mankind. This reminded me of what Sadie Jones wrote in her first novel, *The Outcast,* "There was a stillness like the gap between ticks on a clock, but the ticks never coming."

Life's emptiness enveloped me. I sat spellbound, gaping into this abyss for what seemed hours, but was a few minutes. I felt frozen in time. Perfectly conveyed in the lyrics written by Sarah McLachlan in her song "Time,"

Time here, all but means nothing,

Just shadows that move across the wall.

They keep me company, but they don't ask of me.

They don't say nothing at all.

Suddenly, I was propelled into the awareness of the life around me; the bright lights of the computer room, the heat of the furnace, the endearing presence of my mother's love that permeated her house. My hope for living was renewed. In one split second, I had slipped from the jaws of despair and nothingness back into the land of the living. Feeling alive for the first time in months, I wanted to scream from the rooftop with the exuberance of joy that had flooded my soul.

I was enveloped in the light of God's love. Thus, it was as if the radiance of his love had once again illuminated my life, like the rising of the morning sun, in the brightness of its glory. His presence had delivered me from the pit of despair. My pulse returned to normal. I was like a child on Christmas morning, full of wonder and excitement, suddenly embracing a peace I had only longed for.

Prayers of warriors who had stormed the gates of Heaven had finally pierced through my darkness. In that one bleak moment, God reached His mighty hand down and with great love pulled me back from the pit of despair, like a firebrand plucked from the smoldering fire.

In the downward spiral leading to my suicide attempt, I had allowed my faith to falter. The faith I once had now seemed to be only a memory. In D. Martyn Lloyd-Jones's book, *Faith on Trial,* Lloyd-Jones speaks distinctly, "The one secret is to keep near to God. When we fail, we are like a ship at sea that loses sight of the North Star, or whose compass fails. If we lose our bearings, we must not be surprised at the consequences."

Although true that my faith had been shaken, it is also true to say that my faith had not crumbled. I might have lost sight of the North Star for a brief time, but I was not going to be shipwrecked. I was stubbornly adhering to the promise of *Philippians 1:6,* "Being confident of this very thing, that He which hath begun a good work in you, will perform it until the day of Jesus Christ."

My brother Stan and I are very close. He is also a man of great faith in God. I knew full well his prayers for me, and his faith in God to help me through this turbulent period in my life were reason enough to believe why I was being pulled back from this chasm of despair. Stan is a man like the late Oswald Chambers, "We have to pray with our eyes on God, not on our difficulties."

My faith in God had always been a mainstay of strength and security in my life. This faith had sustained me through many trials and tests, the two greatest of which were my suicide attempt, and the death of my precious mother, Anna Belle. Oftentimes, we come to a point in our faith where it seems we are groping in darkness. We can't seem to see the next step.

One of my favorite psalms conveys this kind of faith. In *Psalms 13:1-2,* the psalmist David cries, "How long wilt thou forget me, O Lord? forever? How long wilt thou hide thy face from me? How long shall I take counsel in my soul, having sorrow in my heart daily?"

"All the powers of his enemies had not driven the Psalmist from his stronghold. As the shipwrecked mariner clings to the mast, so did David cling to his faith; he neither could nor would give up his confidence in the Lord his God. O that we may profit by his example and hold by our faith as to our very life." (Charles Spurgeon, *Spurgeon's Treasure of David.*)

In Philip Yancey's book, *Where Is God When It Hurts?,* he writes, "Meanwhile, where is God? This is one of the most disquieting symptoms. When you are happy, so happy that you have no sense of needing Him, if you turn to Him with praise, you will be welcomed with open arms. But go to Him when your need is desperate, when other help is vain and what do you find? A door slammed in your face, and a sound of bolting and double-bolting on the inside. After that, silence. You may as well turn away." This is the time to trust.

My life is now filled with joy and wonder. I have great goals for my life in the area of suicide prevention and writing my memoir. A quote from Ralph Waldo Emerson is my inspiration, "Do not go where the path may lead; go instead where there is no path and leave a trail."

I am happy to say that almost five years after gaping into this dark chasm of despair, I am whole once again. My hope is to reach those who are fighting this despair in the mind, what the late Dr. Edwin Shneidman referred to as "psych ache," unbearable pain in the mind.

It does get better!

FAITH

"Faith means believing in advance what will only make sense in reverse." Philip Yancey, *Disappointment with God: Three Questions No One Asks Aloud*

On an ordinary day in May 1987, as I prayed on the carpeted floor of my second-floor apartment in Huntington, WV, I received a word from God, through the Holy Spirit.

In His way, the Holy Spirit spoke, "Wait for that that I have given thee. The time of figs has not yet come, but wait, for my time is your time."

Only a few days before, I had returned from a missionary trip to Haiti to face a new direction in life after a failed engagement. A little discouraged, I tried to reassure myself that God was in control. In the four short years I had been a Christian, one thing I had learned was that God's timing was everything.

It's now been over thirty-two years since this divine revelation, and through this vast period, I have come to know a God of great grace and mercy.

Too many times in life we make our plans and ask God to bless them, when all along we should have sought to obey His will. American writer/director Woody Allen is quoted as saying, "If you want to make God laugh, tell him your plans." I concur.

As I look back over my life, I take a long look at the theme of my memoir: finding peace during conflict. Yes, there have been a few deep valleys, but there have been some mountain-top experiences too.

In the profound poem, "Footprints," the poet looks back over his life and reflects on the saddest and darkest times of his life, only to realize that in those dark and sad times, it was then that the Lord carried him. I have come to realize this in my life as well. Madame Jeanne Guyon, a Christian activist in the 17th century, once wrote, "If knowing answers to life's questions is absolutely necessary to you, then forget the journey. You will never make it. For this is a journey of unknowables —or unanswered questions, enigmas, incomprehensibles, and most of all, things unfair."

I know deep in my heart, beyond a shadow of a doubt, I would never have lived to write this chronicle of my life's ups and downs, had I not been given a constant, stubborn faith in my God. Yes, there have been disappointments; yes, there have been dark nights of despair, but I will say with the utmost confidence, the Lord was with me each and every step of the way. He felt every tear I shed, and, according to *Psalm 56:8*, "You have collected all my tears in your bottle…"

In the 12th chapter of 2 *Corinthians* we have the apostle Paul's recollection of one caught up into the third heaven, "and heard unspeakable words which it is not lawful for a man to utter." The apostle goes, "and lest I should be exalted above measure through the abundance of revelations, there was given to me a thorn in the flesh, the messenger of Satan to buffet me, lest I should be exalted about measure. For this thing I besought the Lord thrice, that it might depart from me."

Our faith is a precious gem. As Christian singer Twila Paris has written in her amazing song, "For the Glory of the Lord," "we are made a channel where His grace is poured."

In the hardships we all face in this life, if we put our trust in Christ, one thing we can all count on is the grace of God. I can attest to this as 100% true in my life. Through the darkest of times, times when all I could do was weep, the divine grace of God has been my stay. The Lord Jesus goes on to tell the apostle in 2 *Corinthians 12:9*, "And he said unto me, 'My grace is sufficient for thee: for My strength is made perfect in weakness. Most gladly therefore will I rather glory in my infirmities, that the power of Christ may rest upon me."

If there is anything I have learned in this life, it is that the amazing grace of God is sufficient. In my darkest hour, the strength of my Lord has been there. I will never forget the day my roommate and I had to put our precious Yorkie, Tyler, down. I had gone to visit Tyler on my lunch hour. When I walked back to where he was kept, in an oxygen tent because of his congestive heart failure, I'll never forget as long as I live, how he perked up when he saw me. When I left that day and sat in my car, the hurt of seeing him suffer, knowing that he wasn't going to live long, broke my heart. I couldn't hold back a river of tears that broke loose, and I sat in my car and sobbed.

In that dark moment, as in the moment my precious mother, Anna Belle died, as in the moment I stood at the bathroom sink and saw the reflection of my forlorn face in the mirror as I contemplated suicide, the grace of my Lord Jesus Christ was, and always is, sufficient.

The apostle Paul, when writing to his beloved friend, Timothy, in 2 *Timothy* 2, verse 1, wrote, "Thou, therefore, my son, be strong in the grace that is in Christ Jesus."

My friends, there will be trials and triumphs in this life, this you can be sure of. There will be times when it will take all the strength you can muster to get out of bed. But I promise you, keep going, do what you can, "lift up your eyes unto the hills from whence cometh your help," as David wrote in *Psalm 121*:1.

God is my refuge and strength, and God can be your refuge and strength too! (*Psalm 46*:1)

ABOUT THE AUTHOR

Don Truman Wilson is a writer, spokesperson for suicide prevention and causation, and now the author of the new memoir, *Seeking My Peace in the Midst of Conflict.*

Don's 2009 brush with suicide, though the darkest moment of his life, opened his eyes to see what matters in life as he struggled with same-sex attractions, only to find that the Christian faith he once held so dear nearly died because of the inner conflict. His faith in Christ might have wavered, but it was never lost. He stubbornly refused to give up on his faith as he held to Christ's ever-supporting hand.

A graduate of the Institute for Writers (formerly, the Long Ridge Writers Group), Don has been privileged to work with some of the best writing instructors. He has also strengthened his writing skills by watching the lectures from *The Great Courses*, most notably, "Writing Creative Nonfiction" by Professor Tilar J. Mazzeo, and he is grateful to Professor Mazzeo for her depth and knowledge about writing creative nonfiction.

In January 2018, Don brushed aside the biggest fear he had faced in life and took to the skies above Kennedy Space Center in Merritt Island,

FL, to attempt the first of two skydives. First, he made the 15,000-foot tandem jump; then, in December of 2018, he accomplished the highest tandem jump in the world, the 18,000-foot jump.

After that, Don completed his long-planned memoir, a different kind of scary jump.

Don can be reached by email here: dtrumanwilson@hotmail.com

REVIEW *Seeking My Peace*

Authors and readers benefit greatly from book reviews. It would be appreciated if you would review this book, for example at amazon. com.